French Country Inns & Château Hotels

OTHER BOOKS IN KAREN BROWN'S COUNTRY INN SERIES

ENGLISH, WELSH & SCOTTISH COUNTRY INNS

SWISS COUNTRY INNS & CHALETS

ITALIAN COUNTRY INNS & VILLAS

Scheduled for 1985:

Spanish Country Inns & Paradors

German Country Inns & Castle Hotels

Austrian Country Inns & Castle Hotels

French Country Inns
& Château Hotels

KAREN BROWN

TRAVEL PRESS   San Mateo, California

Illustrations: SHERRY SCHARSCHMIDT, BARBARA TAPP, RICHARD KERR; Cover Design & Painting: BARBARA TAPP; Maps: MARILYN KRIEGER and LORENA BASS; Country Maps and Calligraphy: MARILYN KRIEGER;

TRAVEL PRESS Editors: KAREN BROWN, CLARE BROWN, JUNE BROWN

This book is written as a publication for:

Town and Country Travel Service
16 East Third Avenue, San Mateo, California 94401

International Standard Book Number: 0-930328-09-4
Library of Contress Catalog Card Number: 84-052124
Printed in the United States of America

Distributed by

THE SCRIBNER BOOK COMPANIES, INC.

Travel Press   San Mateo, California

With love to Judy & Carol,

As travels are always more special
when shared with dear friends

MY DEAR FRANCOPHILES:

How I have enjoyed hearing from so many of you who used the earlier editions of *FRENCH COUNTRY INNS & CHATEAU HOTELS* as a companion to your own travels! Although I was not always afforded the time to respond individually to each of your letters, I greatly appreciate your comments, constructive criticisms and interest. Thank you for your thoughtfulness and for giving me the opportunity to vicariously share your experiences along the routes I love so dearly.

Many of your comments regarding specific hotels, descriptions of your own favorites that I unfortunately overlooked, and generous suggestions as to how I might improve *FRENCH COUNTRY INNS & CHATEAU HOTELS* as a guide, most definitely influenced and strengthened this revision. To encourage future comments, I have included a form at the back of this book requesting your opinion of any hotels that you visited based on my recommendation. I would also love to know of your personal favorite or "discovery" to possibly share in future editions. It would be a great help if you could include a brochure and description.

This has been an exciting and important year for Travel Press. I am pleased to share with you the news that the Scribner Book Companies has obtained exclusive trade distribution for our series on European country inns. As my friends say, it seems that Travel Press has finally hit the big time! As a result, the "staff" and series are quickly expanding. *FRENCH COUNTRY INNS & CHATEAU HOTELS* is now in its third edition which includes many sensational new hotels and expanded itineraries; *ENGLISH, WELSH & SCOTTISH COUNTRY INNS* is being completely revised for a new edition; *SWISS COUNTRY INNS & CHALETS* is in its second printing; *ITALIAN COUNTRY INNS & VILLAS* is now on the market and we are busily researching four new inn guides to be released next year on Austria, Germany, Spain and Portugal. We promise to maintain our standards and continue to personally inspect every hotel and provide you with, what we think, are the very finest books on the market today for discriminating travelers.

 THANK YOU, KAREN

Contents

HOTEL SECTION

INDEX

INTRODUCTION

YES, YOU CAN FLY TO PARIS, eat hamburgers, stay in an Americanized hotel and return home safely with stacks of snapshots. If you choose, though, you can travel to France and explore it. You can eat, sleep and drink France, venture off into the country, meet the French, and still return home safe with a load of memories and pleasures as well as snapshots to recall them.

To invite you, hundreds of magnificent chateaux, cozy inns, elegant manors and majestic castles, owned and managed by some of the warmest and most fascinating people, are tucked away in the French countryside. Many of them, built and designed centuries ago as private residences, are in suberb locations, have beautiful surroundings, and, fortunately for the traveler, have been turned into hotels. As travelers, we can take full advantage of this opportunity to live France every minute, twenty-four hours a day.

France has so much to offer the inventive and adventurous traveler. I wanted this book to supply enough information to stimulate the interest of just such people. The French provinces are as different as individual countries and deserve to be visited and explored. Travel time is unfortunately limited and therefore it is important to be familiar enough with a region so that you can plan ahead and know just what is valuable to see and what to omit. To minimize worries and simplify your trip it is also wise to make hotel reservations in advance.

The purpose of this book is not simply to inform you of the fact that these places exist, but to encourage you to explore towns and villages not emphasized on tours and to stay at these inns and, perhaps most of all, to convince you that it is not diffucult to do. This book contains all of the necessary ingredients to make you confident about planning your own trips into the more remote areas of France. With easy to follow itineraries to serve as guidelines, and with a list, pictures and descriptions of over 175 charming accommodations throughout France to choose from, the task of programming your own trip will become a pleasure.

This book is organized in two parts. The first half comprises itineraries, outlined on a day to day basis, with hotel suggestions for overnight stops, to tempt you to venture out of Paris into the countryside. The second half is an alphabetical listing by town of a very selective list of hotels with descriptions, illustrations and factual information provided.

ITINERARIES

I have divided France into sections: Paris by Arrondissement, Normandy, Brittany, the Chateau Country, Dordogne, Basque Country, Gorges du Tarn (Tarn Canyon), Provence, Cote D'Azur, Gorges du Verdon (Verdon Canyon), a Gourmet Itinerary, Alsace and new to this edition Le Lot. For each of these sections I have organized four to six day itineraries, with the exception of Paris by Arrondissement. The itineraries can easily be joined together, enabling you to extend your journey into another region if you have the time. These itineraries can be used as guidelines; depending on your own preference, you might choose to establish yourself at one inn as opposed to three or four in a specific region and branch out from there. Covering the highlights of the regions, these itineraries are set up for touring France by car. To explore the countryside and search out the charming places to stay, there is no comparable way to travel!

MAPS

At the beginning of each itinerary is an outline of the general route to be followed. These are artist renderings and are not intended to replace a good commercial map. To supplement our generalized routings you will need a set of detailed maps. A suggestion would be to purchase a comprehensive selection of both city and regional maps before you depart the United States. If you live in a metropolitain area you should have no problem buying maps. Michelin maps are exceptionally good. If you want to deviate from an itinerary to explore on your own, Michelin marks in green the most scenic or interesting roads. Michelin maps also tie in with their excellent "Green Guides" which are an outstanding reference for sightseeing details, facts and information.

As it is not always easy to locate maps, we recommend "Forsyth Travel Library" as an excellent and very reliable source. If you call or contact them by mail they will send you a catalog of maps and books and often can accommodate special requests or items not advertised on the list. Their address is Forsyth Travel Library, Post Office Box 2975, 9154 West 57th Street, Shawnee Mission, Kansas 66201 and telephone number is (913) 384-3440.

In this book, before the hotel description section is a map of France showing all of the towns in which hotels are recommended. On this map each of the towns is marked with a number indicating its location. These numbers flow geographically across the map to aid you in quickly finding alternate hotels in the area should your first choice be unavailable. These map numbers are cross-referenced in the hotel description section and the index.

HOTEL DESCRIPTIONS

In the second section of this guide is a complete list of hotels that are referenced alphabetically by town. I have included only hotels that I have personally visited at some point in the past couple of years. It is impossible to revisit them all on any particular trip as there are always new regions and hotels to investigate as well, but on each successive journey I try to include as many as I can. I also rely on feedback from you and do try to follow up on any complaints and eliminate any hotels that are not maintaining their quality of service, accommodations and standard of excellence. This guide may not be for everyone, but I believe the number of people who enjoy traveling as I do, taking advantage of everything a country and its people have to offer, is growing. This book is designed for travelers who want to see the French at home, who are willing to conquer their inhibitions and to employ the few phrases remembered from the long-ago, once-a-week language class and who prefer antiques and charm to a guaranteed plumbing system. People who want to add personal experiences to their list of overnight stops will remember the country inns and chateau-hotels included in this book. The hotels might range from luxurious to country-cozy, but they are all charming, quaint and typically French. If you find you can agree with my conditions and are willing to be spoiled as I have been, read on.

HOTEL RATES AND INFORMATION

The French government regulates the hotel rates in France. Prices are published at the beginning of each calendar year and do fluctuate. However, the relative values do not change: from year to year one budget hotel will still be approximately the same cost as another budget hotel and conversly, one luxurious hotel will always be in a similar price range with another deluxe hotel. Therefore, since to accurately quote exact rates is always difficult hotels are referenced by a category of hotel. They are listed as either INEXPENSIVE, MODERATE, EXPENSIVE or VERY EXPENSIVE. Special pricing situations or values are indicated in the text of the description. Also, please note that certain hotels require a minimum stay or that meals be taken at the hotel and are reflected in the room rate. Demi-pension is the French term for Modified American Plan or MAP. This plan includes breakfast and either lunch or dinner in the room rate. Pension is the French term for American Plan or AP which is a plan that includes all three meals. The prices quoted in this case might sound expensive, but usually are an excellent value.

Prices vary and the pleasure is not proportionate to the price. Do not exclude a hotel because the listed prices are high or because they are low. Also, remember that some of the most expensive and elegant hotels have a few reasonably priced bathless rooms tucked away. Do not panic! There is almost always a bath down the hall which you can use for a minimal charge. Just inform the desk that you like to bathe and shortly someone will knock at your door, hand you a bath towel or robe and inform you that your bath is ready and waiting; be spoiled while saving money. But because the prices of French hotels do cover such a wide range, I have based my selection on charm, hospitality, comfort and cleanliness. No matter what the room charge you will find these characteristics a common denominator for every hotel recommended. Of course, for some of you, cost will not be a factor if the hotel is outstanding. For others, budget will guide your choices. What I have tried to do is to indicate what each hotel has to offer, to describe the setting, qualify whether the appeal is simple and rustic or elegant and deluxe, so that you can make the choice to suit your own preferences and holiday. If you know what to expect I believe you will not be disappointed and I have therefore tried to be very honest in the appraisal of each hotel.

CREDIT CARDS

Many small hotels do not accept credit cards. Those hotels which do accept "plastic payment" are indicated in the hotel description section using the following abbreviations: AX = American Express, VS = Visa, MC = Master Charge, DC = Diner's Club, EC = Eurocard, or simply All Major Cards.

CURRENT

You will need a transformer plus an adapter if you plan to take an American made electrical appliance. The voltage in France is 220. Certain outlets are for shavers only. Check with the hotel management before plugging into any outlet to protect both yourself and your appliance.

RESERVATIONS

It is normally not too difficult to find accommodations during the off season (November to March). You should be aware, though, that some hotels are booked all year round while others close in certain seasons. To avoid disappointments it is safer to make reservations in advance. However, it is a double bind as reservations are confining and should you change your plans or itinerary, refunds are often difficult to obtain.

But for those of you who are planning your trip around that special little inn or who like the security blanket of each night preplanned so once you leave home you do not have to worry about where to rest your head each night, there are several options for making reservations which are listed below.

TRAVEL AGENT: A travel agent can be of great assistance - particularly if your own time is valuable.   A knowledgeable agent can handle all of the details of your holiday and "tie" it all together for you in a neat little package including hotel reservations, airline tickets, boat tickets, train reservations, ferry schedules, theatre tickets, etc.   For your airline tickets there will be no service fee, but most travel agencies make a charge for their other services.   The best advice is to talk with your local agent.   Be frank about how much you want to spend and ask exactly what he can do for you and what the charges will be. Although the travel agency in your town might not be familiar with all the little places in this guide, since many are so tiny that they appear in no other major sources, loan them your book - it is written as a guide for travel agents as well as for individual travelers.

TELEPHONE: The most efficient way to secure reservations and finalize your itinerary is to call the hotels directly.   The cost is minimal if you direct dial and you can have your answer immediately.   If space is not available, you can then decide on an alternate.   Ask your local operator about the best time to call for the lowest rates and international dialing instructions.   Do keep in mind the convenience of the hour for the hotels when you do dial.   Avoid the dinner hour and mid-morning when reception is occupied with checking out departing guests.

TELEX: If you have access to a telex machine, this is another efficient way to reach a hotel.   When a hotel has a telex the number has been included in the information under the hotel description.   Again, be sure to be specific as to your arrival and departure dates, number in your party and what type of room you want.   And, of course, be certain to include your telex number for their response.

U.S. REPRESENTATIVE: Some hotels in France have a United States representative through which reservations can be made.   Many of these representatives have a toll free telephone number for your convenience. Please take note that some representatives charge a fee to cover their service or reserve the more expensive rooms, or quote a higher price to protect themselves against currency fluctuations and administrative costs.   Nevertheless, this is an excellent method to secure reservations, and again, wherever applicable, telephone numbers of the various representatives are included in the hotel listings.

LETTER: If you plan early enough in advance, you can write to the hotels directly for your reservations.   However, many of the small hotels in the country are run by French families who do not speak English very well, if at all, and they may have difficulty understanding your requests.   To ensure the type of room you want and a prompt response, I have included a sample letter of correspondence.   This letter, written in English and French, covers standard information needed and used when making reservations.   (Please note: French addresses are long and complicated; when writing for reservations be sure to copy the entire address carefully).

HOTEL NAME & ADDRESS - clearly printed or typed

Messieurs:

Nous voudrions reserver pour _____ Nuit(s)
We would like to reserve for (number of) *night(s):*

A partir du _____ jusqu'au _____
From (date of arrival) *to* (date of departure)

_____ chambre(s) a deux lits
room(s) with two beds

_____ chambre(s) au grand lit
room(s) with double bed

_____ chambre(s) avec un lit supplementaire
room(s) with an extra bed

_____ avec une salle de bains et toilette privee
with a bathroom and private toilet

Nous sommes _____ personnes
We have (number) *of persons in our party*

Veuilliez-vous nous ecrire avec le prix de la chambre(s), et qu'est-ce qu'il
faudra comme deposit. Dans l'attente de votre confirmation, nous prions
d'agreer Messieurs, l'expression de nos sentiments distingues,

Please advise availability, rate of the room, and deposit needed. We will
be waiting for your confirmation and send our kindest regards,

YOUR NAME & ADDRESS - clearly printed or typed

Sample Reservation Letter to Hotel

RESTAURANTS

French cuisine is incomparable in art and price. It is not uncommon to pay more for dinner than for a room. There are ways to save both your money and your appetite for a memorable dinner: fruit and croissants for breakfast; bread, cheese and wine for lunch and an occasional pastry in the afternoon are anything but a sacrifice and can be purchased in grocery stores and patisseries along the way. One word of caution, however, stores customarily close from 12:00 noon to 2:00 p.m. every afternoon, and in small towns from 12:00 noon to 4:00 p.m.. On Mondays most stores are closed all day and only a few are open until noon. Do not wait for hunger pangs; in France you must plan against hunger.

Almost all restaurants have a tourist menu or menu of the day. These are set meals which usually include specialties of the house and are quite good and reasonable. By taking advantage of the house menu you usually begin with a soup or vegetable plate, choose between fish or meat accompanied by potatoes, follow with a salad and end with either dessert or cheese, all for the price of one item if you were to order a la carte. On Sundays, however, only a few restaurants remain open and rarely do they offer a tourist menu.

If you want a quick snack, stop at a bar advertising itself as a "brasserie". Here an omelette, a crepe, various salads or a "croque monsieur", (a ham sandwich grilled with cheese), are normally available, tasty and inexpensive.

REGIONAL FOOD SPECIALTIES

NORMANDY: cheese (camembert, pont l'Eveque, livarot, triple creme), cidres, calvados (apple brandy), asparagus, "tripe a la mode de Caen" (tripe with vegetables), "cotes du porc au calvados" (pork chops cooked in calvados)

NORTHERN FRANCE: (Flanders, Artois, Picardy): sugar, cereals, dairy products, "soupe a la biere" (beer soup), "lapin aux pruneaux" (casseroled rabbit cooked with prunes), "hochepot" (beef and vegetable stew), "tarte a la cassonade" (a carmel tart)

BRITTANY: dairy products, abundant fish, local cidre, "crepes" (sweet pancakes filled with chocolate, fruit, liquers, sugar and butter, or ice cream), "gallettes" (wheat crepes filled with eggs, ham, mushrooms, onions, tomatoes or cheese)

CHAMPAGNE: here the champagne enhances and highlights the local poultry and freshwater fish

ALSACE and LORRAINE: German influenced dishes and portions, sauerkraut, sausages, "quiche lorraine" (cheese, cream, egg and bacon pie)

LOIRE VALLEY: poultry and game, plums, pears, apricots, asparagus, mushrooms, "alose a l'oiselle" (grilled shad with a sorrel sauce), "canard a la solognotte" (roast duck with an onion and tomatoe sauce), "terrine de lapin" (rabbit pate), "gogues" (spiced black pudding), "andouillettes" (sausage made from tripe and light), "meringues a la creme fouette" (meringues with whipped cream), "gateau de Pithiviers" (a marzipan-flavored tart), "tarte des demoiselles Tatin" (apple or peach tart)

BASQUE COUNTRY: Spanish-influenced food and cooking (peppers, garlic, spices, sausages), cheeses (fromage du Pyrenees), "jambon de Bayonne" (raw cured ham), "estouffat Catalan" (braised beef in a red wine and garlic sauxe, "piperade" (an omelette with tomatoes and pimentos)

PROVENCE and the RIVIERA: Here the food is more highly flavored than in the north. Loup is the Mediteranean's prized fish; grown locally are garlic, tomatoes and olives; try "soupe au pistou" (a vegetable, tomatoe, red bean and basil soup), "bouillabaisse" (the famous mixed fish soup from Marseilles), "ratatouille" (a vegetable dish made with tomatoes, squash, eggplant, and red peppers), "gras double a la provencale" (tripe cooked in a tomateo sauce), "salade nicoise" (a delicious salad topped with tomatoes, green peppers, tuna fish, anchovies, black olives, olive oil and vinegar dressing)

BORDEAUX: famous Bordelaise sauce, "entrecote" (steak covered with a sauce of shallots, beef marrow and red wine), "anguilles sautees a la bordelaise" (fried eels in a wine sauce), " agneau a la gasconne" (stuffed braised lamb), "pralines de blaye" (crisp almonds), "soup aux marrons"(soup with a chestnut base), "citrouille sucree" (a pumpkin dessert)

PERIGORD: plums from Agen, oysters from the coast, "truffles" (world sought mushrooms), "pate de foie gras" (a pate made from goose liver), "poulet au pot" (chicken casserole)

AUVERGNE: "truffade de Cantal" (truffle dish), "potee auvergnate" (Hot pot) "coq au vin de Chanturge" (chicken casseroled in Chanturge wine)

RHONE VALLEY: cheeses, gratins, mushrooms (cepes, morilles, bolets, chanterelles), "truite" (trout), "poulet en vessie" (chicken cooked in a pig's bladder)

BURGUNDY: "coq au vin Bourgogne" (chicken stewed with mushrooms and red burgundy wine), "potee bourguignonne" (stew made with salt pork, pig's feet and vegetables), "escargots a la bourguingnonne" (snails in garlic and butter), "meurette" (stew made with eel and red or white wine), "oreillons de veau" (calves ears stuffed with pike and cooked in Chambertin wine), "poulet au Chambertin" (chicken cooked in Chambertin wine), "Pauchouse" (fish stew cooked in white wine with herbs and onions), "quenelles de brochet" (ground poached pike in a cream sauce)

INTERNATIONAL ROAD SIGNS

 End of all restrictions

 Halt sign

 Halt sign

 Customs

 No stopping

 No parking/waiting

 Mechanical help

 Filling station

 Telephone

Camping site

 Caravan site

 Youth hostel

 All vehicles prohibited

 No entry for all vehicles

 No right turn

 No U-turns

 No entry for motorcars

 No overtaking

 Road works

 Loose chippings

 Level crossing with barrier

 Level crossing without barrier

 Maximum speed limit

 End of speed limit

 Traffic signals ahead

 Pedestrians

 Children

 Animals

 Wild animals

 Other dangers

 Intersection with non-priority road

 Merging traffic from left

 Merging traffic from right

 Road narrows

 Road narrows at left

 Road narrows at right

Introduction

ROADS

There are many Auto Routes linking major cities and the French have plans to extend and add a few more. They are wide, beautifully paved, and maintained. They cut distances noticeably. There are also toll roads. If you have unlimited time and a limited budget you may prefer the smaller freeways and country roads. My suggestion would be to definitely use the Auto Routes to navigate in and out or bypass large cities and then, if preferred, return to the country roads.

The extensive road system in France is well groomed and well marked. If you are in the vicinity, there will always be enough road signs to direct you to your destination. By driving the non-toll roads I saw many of the countryside villages bypassed by the Auto Routes. Had I traveled the freeways, my contacts and experiences with the French and their country would have been cut in half. My most enjoyable memories are of the frequent times I would find myself on a country road, alone. The drives through vineyards, orchards and past country or mountain villages were always scenic and I would find myself going as slowly as possible, trying to absorb everything and wanting it to last forever. Often I would share the company of a few bicyclers, herdsmen tending their sheep or cattle, farmers working in the fields, or local inhabitants taking time out to sit at the central cafe for a refreshing or warming drink. The French pace is relaxed, calm and happy and it will influence your driving.

DRIVING TIPS

A valid driver's license is adequate if your stay does not exceed a year, but I would suggest picking up an international driver's license at AAA. Obtaining one is a simple procedure and the cost is quite reasonable.

For finding your way about, Michelin has a wonderful collection of maps that cover small areas and are accurate and detailed. Road numbers, mileage, towns, even isolated hotels and small dirt roads are shown. The most scenic roads are marked in green.   Ignore any specific destinations and simply follow one green line to another; the drive will be exciting and beautiful.   To squeeze the most enjoyment from your holiday, these maps are essential. Please buy the appropriate maps for "your" area before taking to the road. Again, they are not the large ones, but small green sectional maps that can be purchased in tobacco or bookstores ("libraries") throughout France.   They will prove invaluable.   (See section on MAPS for further information.)

The French are aggressive drivers, so be brave.   However, the rules of the road are basically the same; the goal is to arrive at your destination safely and without any collisions!   Just stay in the right lane as much as possible - the left lane is for passing and speed demons.   When you do pass, leave your blinker on for the duration of the act.   Speed limits, if they do exist, are only posted sometimes and generally are ignored when they are.   Cars on the right usually have the right of way. Honking is strictly forbidden in most cities and towns; you are supposed to flash your lights instead.   Paris traffic does demand some practice, nerves and getting used to, but traffic between, in and around the smaller cities and towns should not present much of a problem.   Gas stations are numerous enough so that you should never have to worry about running out of petrol.   They might appear closed or empty, but have patience ... the owner has most likely just disappeared for a moment to talk with a friend at the neighboring store or local bar.

I know France because I literally drove it from one corner to the other. If you really want to travel in France, you cannot just jump from one town to village to city; it is just as important to see the countryside inbetween.

I have spent now almost twelve months investigating hotels, becoming familiar with the provinces and researching for this book.   With several hotels to visit every day, I was continuously on the move.   My experiences, both good and bad, frightening and exciting, are invaluable to me.   The French people I encountered and came to know where anything but "cold".   They are a very hospitable, warm, intelligent and proud people.   They are as wonderful as their country is beautiful.   I have included over 175 hotels in this book where you can stay and have them prove it to you themselves.

NORMANDY

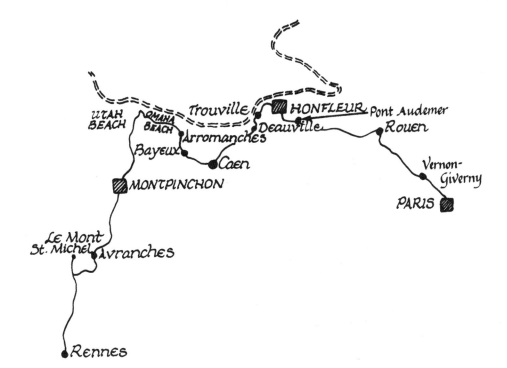

UTAH BEACH

OMAHA BEACH

Trouville

HONFLEUR

Pont Audemer

Deauville

Rouen

Arromanches

Bayeux

Vernon-Giverny

Caen

MONTPINCHON

PARIS

Le Mont St. Michel

Avranches

Rennes

THIS ITINERARY TAKES YOU TO the well known D-Day beaches, where on June 6, 1944, American and British troops landed in a major and dramatic attempt to change the pace of World War II.   Decades have passed since then, but many towns are still struggling to recover and restore the damage. Pill boxes, although abandoned, remain strategically positioned along the deserted beaches and many vivid memories and tragic losses have yet to be forgotten.

The D-Day beaches are but one small section of the Normandy coastline and region.   Normandy calls to mind the Vikings and their invasions as well as William the Conqueror and his.   It is also dairies, isolated and beautiful stud farms, mile after mile of rolling green pastures and picturesque resort areas.   When following your course towards the D-Day beaches you will pass through a bit of everything.

Day I   HONFLEUR   La Ferme Saint Simeon

===

Begin your day with what might well prove the highlight of your trip.   Follow the Seine north out of Paris to VERNON and GIVERNY, Monet's beautifully restored house, studio, greenhouse, lilypads and gardens.   Here he lived and created masterpieces.   Walk the gardens and discover the enchantment of the lilypads ... all to understand what inspired the brilliance of the artist.   Pack a lunch and take advantage of the fact that for a small fee one can linger and enjoy what has to be one of the world's most magnificent picnic spots!

It is not a long drive from Paris to the capital and heart of Normandy, the city of ROUEN.   Rouen itself is one of the most important tourist centers of northern France.   William the Conqueror died here in 1087 and Joan of Arc was burned at the stake in the Place du Vieux Marche in 1431.   Although the city was practically destroyed during World War II, it still has many interesting museums and its famous cathedral, so well known to many from Monet's paintings.

Not far from Rouen, deep in the Normandy countryside, is the tanners' town of PONT AUDEMER. It is also the town that the father of William the Conqueror stormed. In spite of the war's destruction, the town managed to salvage a number of old timbered houses which line the Rue de la Licorne. For me, Pont Audemer also means the location of a cozy inn, L'AUBERGE DE VIEUX PUITS, marvelous food and the kind couple who own it, M and Mme Jacques Foltz. If you are the least bit hungry, it will serve as a wonderful stopping place for lunch.

The next and final destination for today is the picturesque harbor town of HONFLEUR. The narrow, 17th century harbor with its many colorful boats is outlined by numerous, well-preserved old timbered houses. Honfleur is the birthplace of the humorist Alphonse Allais, the musician Erik Satie and the painter Eugene Boudin. There is a unique wooden church and the house of the King's lieutenant, all this is left of a 16th century Chateau. Wander and explore the streets remembering that you can return again tomorrow morning after your first wonderful night at LA FERME SAINT SIMEON.

Normandy

This hotel is not more than a mile around the peninsula from Honfleur. It is a typical Norman timbered farm house, with flower baskets at each window. It was purchased not too many years ago by a young couple who strive to meet your every need. I have some friends who ventured out from the Charles de Gaulle airport through fog and who arrived six hours later than anticipated. Well past midnight, the Boelen's were still up waiting to greet their guests.

Le Ferme Saint Simeon is an excellent hotel and you should consider it "home" for the two nights you anchor here. The dining room is cheerful with yellow walls, bright yellow table cloths and colorful flower arrangements. The cuisine is plentiful and delicious although expensive-everything is a' la carte. There are only ten rooms, nine apartments and every one is handsomely decorated with fine antiques. Reservations are a must and should be made long in advance.

Day II   HONFLEUR   La Ferme Saint Simeon

Today is for visiting Honfleur again if you wish and the other active seaside resorts. Favorite scenes for many impressionist artists, particularly Monet and Renoir, you might feel as if you have already seen this particular stretch of Normandy coastline if you have spent any time in the Jeu de Paume Museum in Paris.

TROUVILLE is responsible for setting the pace on the "Cote de Fleurie." It has been popular since 1852. A stretch of water divides its very close neighbor, DEAUVILLE. Deauville is perhaps the most elegant resort of them all. Internationally popular, dazzling and luxurious, every variety of entertainment is to be found here. Locate here in the late summer and experience the excitement and sophistication of a major summer playground for the rich and famous. For a few glamourous weeks each August there is the allure of the racetracks, polo fields, luncheons and black tie dinners!

Celebrities and the wealthy international set are here to cheer their prize thoroughbreds on. Get a relaxed glimpse of these million dollar babies as they "limber up" with an early morning stretch along Deauville's glorious expanse of sandy beach.

Spend the day touring the resort coastal towns. Stroll, hike or just wander, watch the lovely coastal sunset and then it is time to go "home" to dinner.

Day III   MONTPINCHON   Chateau de la Salle

To devote an entire day to exploring the landing beaches, depart early from La Ferme Saint Simeon.

The first stop is CAEN. Situated on the banks of the Orne, it lost nearly all of its 10,000 buildings in the Allied invasion of 1944. A large city, it is a port and is also the city that William the Conqueror made his seat of government. Northwest of Caen is BAYEUX, an ancient Roman Metropolis. Once a capital of ancient Gaul, this city was successfully invaded by the Bretons, the Saxons and the Vikings but somehow escaped the Allied invasions which brought with them so much destruction. As a result the town still possesses Norman timbered houses, stone mansions and cobble-stoned streets. It also where the famous Bayeaux Tapestry is displayed. Commissioned in England it portrays in graphic detail the Battle of Hastings in 1066 in 58 dramatic scenes. From Bayeux, the road intersects with the route that winds along the coast following its curves and the D-Day beaches.

ARROMANCHES LES BAINS was a small fishing port until the British took it over in order to install an artificial harbor to supply the Allied forces. Mulberry was the name of that harbor, and its wreckage lies right off the beach. Arromanches is also the location of an interesting museum where a film is shown of the 1944 invasion and landings. It will refresh facts in your mind and set the mood for visiting the beaches yourself. As you continue, stop every so often to walk on the beaches, explore the pill boxes and reconstruct in your mind what took place on June 6, 1944.

Further along the coast is OMAHA BEACH, where the wreckage of the war can still clearly be seen. The Americans occupied this beach on the 6th of June. Omaha was the code name which had previously referred to the three beaches in the area: ST. LAURENT, VIERVILLE SUR MER, and COLLEVILLE. In the vicinity of these three beach towns are many memorials. A monument marks the temporary burial spot for those first to fall in the Battle of the Beaches. In the sector of Omaha Beach known as Dog Green seventy per cent of the 116th Regiment were either dead or wounded within minutes of landing. UTAH BEACH, a short distance away, was another landing spot for the American forces.

With thoughts, visions and memories occupying your mind, drive towards MONTPINCHON and the CHATEAU DE LA SALLE. Here you will find quiet, privacy and time to piece everything together. A more appropriate address for the secluded chateau might be "somewhere in the country." Once a private estate, it is a stone mansion that has only ten bedrooms. All are large, handsomely decorated and have either a bath or a shower. The restaurant has a few heavy wooden tables positioned before a warming fire and is small enough so that it is not overwhelming. The cuisine and the fire will tempt you to linger over specialities such as "timbale de vis de veau."

Day IV

Pass through AVRANCHES this morning. It was here on July 30, 1944, that General Patton began his attack against the German Panzer counter-offensive from Mortaim.

From Avranches cross into Brittany to the famous French town of LE MONT SAINT MICHEL. One of France's proudest possessions, Le Mont Saint Michel is unique, dramatic and definitely a site to visit. The magnificent city is built on a rock 235 feet high and, depending on the tide, is either surrounded by water or by exposed quicksand. Wander up the narrow cobble-stoned streets to the crowning Twelfth Century abbey and visit the remarkable Gothic and Romanesque complex. Imagine William the Conqueror at prayer before the invasion of Britain, or a recitation of the "Chanson de Roland." Saint Michel, the militant archangel, is the appropriate saint for the beaches you have just seen. Savour an omelette made famous by Mme Poulard at the Hotel Mere Poulard. The preparation is an attraction on its own merit. The eggs are whisked at a tempo and beat set by the chef himself and then cooked in copper pans over an open fire.

From Le Mont Saint Michel it is approximately an hour's drive south to the city of RENNES, and to various other means of transportation. From here you can easily return to Paris, or if tempted, journey, on into the region of Brittany.

BRITTANY

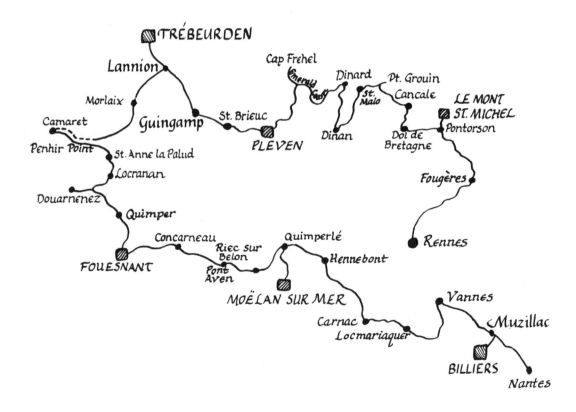

TRÉBEURDEN

Lannion

Cap Fréhel

Dinard

Pt. Grouin

Emerald Coast

St. Malo

Cancale

LE MONT ST. MICHEL

Morlaix

Guingamp

St. Brieuc

Dinan

Dol de Bretagne

Pontorson

Camaret

PLEVEN

Penhir Point

St. Anne la Palud

Fougères

Locranan

Douarnenez

Quimper

Quimperlé

Concarneau

Riec sur Belon

Hennebont

Rennes

FOUESNANT

Pont Aven

MOËLAN SUR MER

Vannes

Carnac

Muzillac

Locmariaquer

BILLIERS

Nantes

BRITTANY IS A REGION OF BEAUTIFUL forests bounded by nearly a thousand miles of coastline.   A peninsula jutting out from the northwest side of France, it is, geographically, an area very easy to distinguish.   Culturally it also carries its own distinct personality.   The regional language is Breton and traditional costumes are proudly worn by the inhabitants.   Crepes or Galettes, which are crepes without sugar, filled with ham, eggs or cheese; fish and cidre (carbonated apple juice) are Brittany's specialities.   Houses are all of a similar construction and style.   They are fresh white stucco and angled blue-gray roofs.   Windmills pop up every so often on the crest of a hill and the people are friendly and their French carries a distinctive accent.

The city of NANTES and the famous town, LE MONT SAINT MICHEL mark the beginning and the end of this spectacular region.   This itinerary generally follows Brittany's coastline from one point to the other.   Each coastal town on the tour is too fascinating to miss.   The wooded interior, although not emphasized on this particular itinerary, is also very beautiful and should not be overlooked especially if camping, horseback riding or hiking interest you.

DAY I   LE MONT ST MICHEL   Hotel Le Mere Poulard

Your tour begins at RENNES, the administrative and cultural capital of Brittany. It is a large commercial city but Vieux Rennes or the old part of town is composed of quaint narrow streets which are lined by dignified old timbered houses.   From Rennes drive north towards FOUGERES.   Of interest here is a magnificent feudal castle with thirteen large towers isolated on an island.

Another twenty miles or so of driving and you arrive at LE MONT SAINT MICHEL.   Here you are.   The mount has been photographed by millions and talked about all over the world.   It is the militant Archangel Michael's domain.   The fantastic city-church is built on a rock, like the Mother Church, but this one is 235 feet high.   The appearance of the city is that of a child's sand castle.   Narrow, cobbled-stoned streets wind up to the Twelfth Century abbey at the top in the center of the city.   The Gothic and Romanesque complex is made accessible to the public by an elevated roadway.   Le Mont St. Michel is famous for the extreme tide levels which occur daily.   At different intervals, according to the type of tide, the city is either completely surrounded by water or by exposed quicksand.   Check the tide schedule and then choose a restaurant where you can enjoy a meal or snack and watch the amazing and dramatic tide changes.

The home of M and Mme Bernard Heyraud is also the HOTEL MERE POULARD, enabling you to stretch out your stay on this isolated city.   The rooms, although not extremely large, are comfortable and simply furnished. The hotel also has a cheery and bright restaurant which is famous for its Poulard omelette.

Glance back once more at Le Mont St. Michel, securing it in your memory and then drive south to Pontorson and DOL-DE-BRETAGNE, the capital of the marshland, and then east along the coastline.   Heading for St. Malo you pass through VIVIER, a large mussel producing area, CANCAL, a picturesque seaside resort, and POINT GROUIN where you can enjoy a sweeping panorama from CAP FREHEL across to Le Mont St. Michel.   It is here at Point Grouin that the beautiful EMERALD COASTLINE begins.

ST. MALO, known as the city of corsairs, was once the lair of pirates. Its setting is unique and has become an important tourist center.   The city was destroyed by a Nazi-set fire at the time of their 1944 invasion, but the 13th and 14th century ramparts that surround the town have since been restored.   South of St. Malo is the walled town of DINAN, a must to see.   Once inhabited by the Dukes of Normandy, the town has a very old appearance.   Dinan is known for its houses built on stilts over the streets and the remnants of its once fortified chateau.   DINARD lies only twenty-two miles north of Dinan.   A popular resort, Dinard is in a lovely area and has many safe and protected beaches.   The Emerald Coast between Dinard and Cap Frehel is quite impressive, jagged and beautiful.

Not far from this wild coastline is another main attraction equally as beautiful, but calm: LE MANOIR DE VAUMEDEUC.   Located twelve miles from the coast in the Hunaudaye Forest, this 15th century manor has a peaceful environment and has retained its medieval flavor.   Le Manoir is an excellent hotel managed by Mme Pontbriand.   She and her personnel create a genial, home-like feeling.   There are ten handsome bedchambers.   Furniture, elegant tapestries, paintings, beamed ceilings, views, and small items in each room (a chest filled with antique odds and ends, a case of colorful lead soldiers) catch your attention and provide a hint of the special quality which makes Le Manoir de Vaumedeuc unique.   Personal touches are found everywhere and add just that much more warmth and richness to an atmosphere already so.   Whether you will spend more of your time here in the coziness of your private bedroom, in one of the   comfortable sitting rooms or in the intimate dining room sampling marvelous cuisine must be your own decision.

DAY III   TREBEURDEN   Ti Al Lannec

There are many adventures on the itinerary today so your departure from Le Manoir de Vaumedeuc must, unfortunately, be an early one.   The relatively long drive for today is through such beautiful country that the length will not be noticed by even the most impatient travelers.

It is approximately thirty miles to ST. BRIEUC, one of the most important industrial centers of the region.   Located on a bay, should you wish to tackle this large city, there are many pretty walks to take, old mansions and majestic townhouses to discover.   Also do not miss the fortified cathedral of St. Stephen and the 15th century fountain.

The drive continues now to one of the northernmost tips of the Breton coastline. A very popular seaside location the small town of TREBEURDEN is lovely. Set on the hills above the coast the views out to the Grande, Molene and Milliau islands are striking on a clear day. Yachts anchor off the scattered stretches of sandy beach and dear shops line the few main shopping streets to cater to the summer vacationers. Let the season and weather determine your length of stay here. But regardless of whether or not the sun shines there is a charming hotel perched on a point that is convenient to the beaches in warm weather and cozy on a dreary, dark, gray day.

The   TI AL LANNEC achieves a feeling of "home away from home", from the smell of croissants baking to the personal touches in the decor. The restaurant is lovely and opens onto glorious views of the coast. The public rooms have been thoughtfully equipped to accommodate the hobbies of the guests and the unpredictable moods of the weather. There were jigsaw puzzles, books, games, in addition to a swingset on the lawn and an outdoor, knee-high chess set. Gerard et Danielle Jouanny are responsible for the careful renovation of this once private home and Madame Jouanny's feminine touch is apparent in the sweet choice of prints that decorate the majority of rooms. The bedrooms are truly individual, but all extremely comfortable for extended stays and have bright modern bathrooms. Most of the rooms look out to the sea. This is a hotel for vacationing families and one to which I would most definitely like to return.

DAY IV   FORET FOUESNANT   Manoir Du Stang

With a full day ahead of you an early start is again needed. Back-track to Lannion and then head south to take the road which follows the coastline out to the very tip of the peninsula and the lobster port of CAMARET. In the area there are many scenic points and the most beautiful of them all is PENHIR POINT. Pass through STE. ANNE PALUD, one of the most frequented pilgrimage centers in Brittany, to the quaint village LOCRANAN. Now known for its woodcarvers, it once was called the "city of weavers" when three hundred workers gathered there to weave sails for the British navy. Located on the square is a group of lovely Renaissance houses. DOUARNENEZ, a lively sardine fishing port lies to the west of Locranan and QUIMPER, a city famous for its pottery, lies to the south.

From Quimper it is only ten miles further south to FOUESNANT, a cider producing city in a green setting, and to the marvelous 16th century manor house, MANOIR DU STANG. This private home is so cozy, the cuisine so delicious and the owners so accommodating that you might decide to spend the rest of your vacation here. The owner describes it as "not really a small hotel or inn but it should be considered more as our own comfortable family home where we receive guests." Perhaps it is this attitude and the sincerity of it that stimulate the raves and strong recommendations always associated with this hotel. The manor is surrounded by flower gardens, a small lake, woods and acres of farmland. The furnishings retain the feeling of a private estate, yet the rooms have all the modern conveniences and comforts. The Louis XV styled dining room is romantic and the food always hearty and good.

DAY V   MOELAN SUR MER   Moulin du Duc

For those of you who are impatient to see what is in store for you today, and indeed you have every reason to be, note that your first stop, CONCARNEAU, is only a few miles away. An old port, this walled city has houses dating from the 14th century. As with almost all Breton seaside villages, Concarneau also has its share of white sand beaches. Continuing on through the peaceful market village of Pont Aven, it is a short distance to the small town RIEC SUR BELON where flat shelled oysters and the charming HOTEL CHEZ MELANIE are found.

You might want to lunch here; the food is delicious, and you will be graciously served by young maidens traditionally costumed.   Drive further to the village of QUIMPERLE.   Along the Laita River are some unbelievable old homes.

Any disappointments you might still have concerning the departure from the Manoir du Stang this morning are guaranteed to disappear upon arrival at LE MOULIN DU DUC, located only six miles south of Quimperle at MOELAN SUR MER.   By a small lake with lilypads, ducks, and a few colorful rowboats, is the quaint old hotel, formerly a mill.   The dining here is exquisite, the owners are charming and the service is wonderful.   The attractive rooms with modern conveniences are in annexes found alongside the babbling stream.

Last day in Brittany, and every moment is precious and needed!

Return to Quimperle and then continue on through the once fortified town of HENNEBONT.   Next you arrive at the small town of CARNAC, another seaside resort.   Carnac is where you will find the field famous for its megaliths. Similar to England's Stonehenge, these huge stones are an important prehistoric find and yet they appear scattered and abandoned in an open field.   There are no fences to restrict your explorations nor stands with postcards and momentos. However, at the far end of the site is a cafe where you can sample some of the Breton galettes, crepes and cider.   A short distance away at LOCMARIAQUER are two additional prehistoric stones: the Merchant's table and the Great Menhir.

Return to the main road from Vannes to Nantes and detour at Muzillac to travel out to the tip of the Pen-lan peninsula and the small village of BILLIERS.   Here on a rocky promontory is a hotel that will leave you with a lasting impression of Brittany.   In 1978 Patrick Gasnier "et sa brigade" took charge of the DOMAINE DE ROCHEVILAINE and it has dramatically improved under his care and supervision.   The bedrooms are handsomely furnished and beautifully appointed.   The vast windows of the dining room expose the rocky cliffs.   There is a distinctive sensation of being shipboard ... all you see from the table is the wild open sea.   Beautiful oriental carpets adorn hardwood floors and on sunny days breakfast is enjoyed by many in the well kept gardens that are protected from salt water breezes by white washed walls.

The Domaine de Rochevilaine is dramatically positioned on Brittany's jagged and rocky coastline.   The views from the hotel are stupendous with the sun shining and the sea glistening; or, on a stormy day when the wind whips and the waves crash against the rocks so near your bedroom window.   The setting of this hotel exagerates Brittany's most spectacular quality ... its coastline, and it seems a perfect choice for your last destination.

Return to the main road and it is a direct route to either VANNES or NANTES. The capital city, Vannes was constructed around the Cathedral of St. Peter and consists largely of ancient houses within 13th and 15th century ramparts. It is a straight line from Vannes to Nantes where your tour of Brittany ends. Nantes was Brittany's capital from the 10th to the 15th centuries. It has a beautiful old quarter, and is the location of the Duke's Palace, the Cathedrals of St. Peter and of St. Paul, and remains today an important city of the region.

Brittany

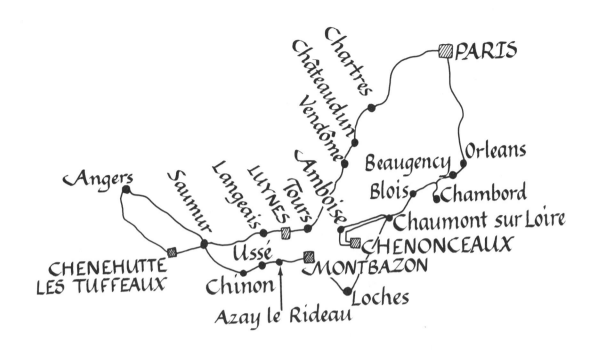

PARIS

Chartres
Châteaudun
Vendôme
Chartres
Beaugency
Orleans
Blois
Chambord
Amboise
Chaumont sur Loire
CHENONCEAUX

Angers
Saumur
Langeais
LUYNES
Tours

CHENEHUTTE
LES TUFFEAUX
Ussé
MONTBAZON
Chinon
Loches

Azay le Rideau

CHÂTEAU
COUNTRY

BEGIN A JOURNEY AT PARIS TO see and experience the beauty and elegance of France's chateaux along the banks of the Loire River. Also known as the "garden of France", the chateaux conjure up the grandeur and excitement of life at the French Court.

DAY I   LUYNES   Domaine de Beauvois

An hour southwest of Paris is the city of CHARTRES and its magnificent cathedral. Monopolizing the horizon, the gothic cathedral is dedicated to Mary, the Mother. Its feminine qualities are best evidenced by its amazing stained-glass windows filling the church with color and light. The cathedral is considered by many to be the greatest achievement of the Middle Ages. It is a "stone testament" of that period.

From Chartres continue south to TOURS and the Loire River. Although without a chateau, Tours, located at the junction of the Cher and Loire Rivers has played an important role in history.

On the north bank of the Loire river, drive east to the small town of LUYNES and the DOMAINE DE BEAUVOIS. Your first chateau on the Loire, you can go one step beyond just visiting it, you may stay here for the night. It is the choice of many who decide to spend some time in the Loire Valley. Recommendations of the guests are always high and there are a great many who return. The Fifteenth Century chateau with its Seventeenth Century "improvements" is surrounded by a wooded estate of 200 acres. It has forty magnificent rooms and a lovely heated pool. Spoil yourself as did the Lords and Ladies who flocked to the Loire Valley in ages past; savor the marvelous entrees topped by a superb strawberry souffle; sit back and dream...

DAY II   CHENEHUTTE LES TUFFEAUX   Le Prieure

CHATEAU DE LANGEAIS, although one of the smaller chateaux in this region, is beautifully furnished and well worth a visit. Built in the Fifteenth Century, it was completed in a period of four to five years and since then has been left intact. The history of the castle, however, dates back to the Ninth Century when the dreaded "Black Falcon", Foulques Nerra, built the first dungeon in Europe. Only the ruins remain to be seen.

Drive further east to the town of SAUMUR, which lies directly on the river's edge. The CHATEAU DE SAUMUR, once a fairy tale castle, no longer possesses such charm as it turrets and towers have long since been destroyed. The castle is strategically located above the town overlooking the Loire. The town itself is very picturesque, set in a region of vineyards famous for their "mousseux" or sparkling wines.

On the outskirts of the chateau region is ANGERS, extending over both the banks of the maine. It is the former capital of the Dukes of Anjou. The original castle, built by Fougeres, was destroyed and then repaired by Saint Louis. Louis IX used the castle as a prison from 1230 until 1238 and the outer walls and the seventeen towers, which remain today, were constructed during this period.

LE PRIEURE in CHENEHUTTE LES TUFFEAUX is tonight's hotel. This is a first class hotel with a fantastic 40-mile wide panorama of the Loire. There they seem to have forgotten that the days of nobility are past.   All the guests are treated and served as if they were the King and Queen themselves. For dinner a pleasing choice would be "grenadin de saumon", a proven specialty.

DAY III   MONTBAZON   Domaine de la Tortiniere

This morning continue west and this time follow the road along the south bank of the Loire river.   The first stop is CHINON, whose fortress chateau is one of the oldest in France.   It is interesting to see the skelton of the castle, but be prepared to fill in large chunks of the interior with your imagination.   The castle is made up of three distinct fortresses, Fort Saint Georges, Chateau de Millieu, and Chateau du Coudray, each separated by deep moats.   It was here that Charles VII based his government from 1429 to 1450, and where Joan of Arc sought the Dauphin.

USSE is the next destination. The Castle of Usse, located in the dark forest of Chinon overlooking the Indre, is everything you would expect a true castle to be. It has steeples, turrets, towers, chimneys, dormers and enchantment. It is believed to be the castle that inspired Perault to write Sleeping Beauty.

AZAY LE RIDEAU and its elegant Renaissance chateau are not far from Usse. The Chateau Azay le Rideau is situated on a small island in the Indre and was so beautifully designed and built in 1518 by Gilles Berthelot, the financial minister of Francois Ier, that the King himself took possession. The memory of this ornate chateau reflecting in the water and framed by whispy trees will remain with you forever.

DOMAINE DE LA TORTINIERE in Montbazon, tonight's hotel, equals if not surpasses any of the chateaux seen today. The chateau has a fine and intricate structure, a lovely pool, grounds designed for romantic strolls, elegant bedrooms decorated with an emphasis on comfort and a superb restaurant. Each evening a delicious menu is created by the chef in addition to the "a la carte" selection. Use your own superlatives...

Chateau Country

The first castle to be seen this morning is LOCHES.   The town of Loches, found in the hills along the banks of the Indre, is often referred to as the "City of Kings."   The ancient castle built during the reign of Charles VII is the "Acropolis of the Loire" and the buildings around it form what is called "Haute Ville."   Here you will find a copy of the proceedings of Joan of Arc's trial. Also Agnes Sorel, renowned for her beauty, was buried in the tower, her portrait can be found in one of the rooms.

From Loches drive to the lovely CHATEAU DE CHAUMONT SUR LOIRE.   Built by Charles D'Amboise during the reign of Louis XII, the chateau was given to Diane de Poitiers by Catherine de Medici in exchange for Chenonceaux.   Surrounded by a beautiful park, it has a lovely position overlooking the Loire.

Any difficulties about leaving Chaumont Sur Loire should disappear with the knowledge that only a few miles west is another beautiful chateau, CHATEAU D'AMBOISE.   It was the first chateau in France to feel the impact of the Italian Renaissance.   It is here in Amboise that Leonardo de Vinci spent his last years and is also the center of the famous vineyards known as Touraine Amboise.

A trip to the Loire Valley would lose all significance if the CHATEAU DE CHENONCEAUX, only a few miles south of Amboise, were omitted from the itinerary.   It gracefully spans the lazy Eure River and is known as the "Chateau of the Six Women": Catherine de Briconnet, the builder; Diane de Poitiers, the ever-beautiful; Catherine de Medici, the magnificent; Louise de Lorraine, the inconsolable; Madame Duphin, lover of letter; and Madame Peolouze, lover of antiquity.   The rooms and bedchambers, elegantly and lavishly furnished, are fun to slowly wander through to avoid missing even the smallest detail.

If you cannot bear the thought of parting, the lovely small HOTEL DU BON LABORADEUR ET DU CHATEAU is nearby and enables you to linger over the charm and enchantment of the most elegant chateau on the Loire for a least another night.   A friendly welcome has now become a tradition for the Jeudin family.   The gastronomic splendors of their table and the comfort and calm of their rooms will convince you that they know how to provide the delights you love to discover... and remember.

DAY V

This morning retrace your steps back past Amboise and Chaumont sur Loire and continue on to BLOIS.   This is the location of the Thirteenth Century chateau constructed by the royal Orleans family.   Most interesting are the magnificent Francois Ier stairway; Catherine de Medici's bedchamber with its many secret wall panels used, in the true Medici tradition, to hide jewels, documents and poisons; and the King's bedchamber where the murder of the Duke de Guise occurred.

The largest of the chateaux has been saved for the last.   CHAMBORD, although almost bare of furniture, retains its grandeur and enchantment especially at sunset or in the deep morning mist.

The last stretch along the Loire before turning north towards Paris takes you through BEAUGENCY and then ORLEANS.   Beaugency is an ancient town noted for its Notre Dame church.   Orleans is famous for the siege led by Joan of Arc.

The drive is now to Paris.   The fabulous city is both end and beginning.

DORDORGNE

Limoges

Cognac

Angoulême

CHAMPAGNAC
DE BELAIR

Brantôme

Bourdeilles

Perigueux

VARETZ

Brive

Dordogne

Libourne

Bordeaux

Bergerac

TREMOLAT

Limeuil

Les
Eyzies

Sarlat

Souillac

Dordogne

Beynac

La Roque

Domme

Rocamadour

GRAMAT

THE DORDOGNE: SLEEPY COUNTRY ROADS, ROLLING green hills and mountains dressed with vineyards and ornamented by magnificent chateaux that conveniently appear on the horizon as the previous one fades away. Groves of aspen and birch blaze in the sunlight and a sleepy river narrows, broadens, and winds tying it all together. This itinerary takes advantage of the Bordeaux wine region and then follows the Dordogne River passing through lovely villages along the way.

DAY I   CHAMPAGNAC DE BELAIR   Moulin du Roc

Starting point is the city of BORDEAUX. It is an important port and a beautiful French city. The old section is jammed with shops and decorated with ornate fountains and old churches. The name, Bordeaux, also implies the largest fine wine district on earth: the red wine districts to the north, the Medoc immediately to the south, and all of the country along the north bank of the Dordogne and facing the Medoc across the Gironde. Most of the white wine is grown in the region between the two rivers, an area called "entre deux mers."

Today will be spent visiting this region, its marvelous chateaux and their cellars, enjoying what it has to offer. Leave Bordeaux for LIBOURNE, the center for the wines of ST. EMILION, POMEROL and FRONSAC. If wine pleases your palate, there are many cellars in the vicinity to sample. Chateau Videlot lies between Libourne and St. Emilion. It is a beautiful house and the owner, M Jean Pierre Moueix is a true wine connoisseur. Neighboring the town of St. Emilion are two noteworthy chateaux. Chateau Ausone is the more famous, where you can walk into a ground floor cellar with a ceiling of vines. Chateau Cheval Blanc, painted a refreshing cream color, produces some of the most splended full-blooded red wine. It is generally agreed that Chateau Petrus is one of the most outstanding vineyards of the Pomeral district.

COGNAC is the name of both a small town and of the brandy made from champagne. The Charente Vineyards, now given over exclusively to cognac, originally produced inferior wines sold to seamen from Britain and the Low Countries who ventured here to buy salt. It was only in the 17th century that some of these immigrants began "burning" the wine, and once the experiment had been made the word quickly spread. In and around Cognac there are a number of distilleries and warehouses. Those of Hennessy and Martell are two of the best known. From Cognac continue east towards ANGOULEME. Begun by the Romans, the upper part of the town is surrounded by ramparts.

Sleepy with wine you'll be glad to know that the MOULIN DU ROC awaits you a short distance from Angouleme. Tucked off a small country road on the outskirts of CHAMPAGNAC DE BELAIR this dear mill remains one of my favorite inns in all of France. It is a small 17th and 18th century stone mill. The eight rooms, although not large are each enchanting. The bathrooms are all modern. Windows overlook the lazy Drome river, the gardens and the beautiful birch lined pastures. The waterside setting is so peaceful and relaxing. The dining room is small and captivating. Madame Gardillou is responsible for the kitchen and the cusine is superb. Monsieur Gardillou serves as a most gracious and charming host. Le Moulin du Roc is a gem!

DAY II   TREMOLAT   Le Vieux Logis

This morning country roads will direct you to the heart of the Dordogne.
Discovered on my countryside tour after the publication of the first edition of
FRENCH COUNTRY INNS & CHATEAU HOTELS I was genuinely charmed by
the village of BRANTOME and the neighboring village of BOURDEILLES.
Bounded by the River Dronne, Brantome is a very pretty town and its ancient
abbaye enhances the picture. Founded by Charlemagne in 769, the abbey was
reconstructed in the 11th century after it was ransacked by the Normans. The
church and adjoining buildings were constructed and modified between the 14th
and 18th centuries. Follow the valley of the Dronne just a few miles further to
Bourdeilles. Crowned by its 12th century castle, Bourdeilles bridges the river

and is a small but charming town to explore. Should you wish to lunch in the area the only problem is that there are too many outstanding choices. I'll offer a few suggestions and leave the chore of choosing to you! (Of course one can always picnic!) In the town of Brantome, MOULIN DE L'ABBAYE, another mill has an exceptional restaurant and being on the water's edge, has a gorgeous outlook. In Bourdeilles, HOTEL DES GRIFFONS has a lovely restaurant and the chef is flattered if you request regional specialties.

From Brantome continue on to PERIGIEUX, an interesting old city, and arrive at BERGERAC, a town directly on the river and reputedly Cyrano's home. From here the road parallels the Dordogne and as the road nears TREMOLAT, the stopping point for today, the valley becomes more gentle and lush.

LE VIEUX LOGIS ET SES LOGIS DES CHAMPS is an ideal base from which to explore one of France's loveliest regions. The character of Le Vieux Logis matches the beauty of the valley. Opening up on one side to farmland, this charming hotel also has its own little garden in back with a narrow stream and various small bridges. The rooms, recently redone, are perfectly color coordinated down to the smallest detail. In room # 10 everything is in large red and white checks: The comforters, the pillows, the curtains, the canopy. The restaurant is located in the barn, and the tables are cleverly positioned within each of the stalls. Take a stroll after dinner and wander through the sleepy tobacco growing village of Tremolat. The lofty barns lay open and hang heavy with tobacco. The town's church is also one of the oldest in the area and has a lovely stained glass window.

Linger in this region for as many days as your itinerary affords, use Tremolat as your base and let the river be your guide. Discover the beauty of the Dordogne by driving the quiet roads and simply happening upon the peaceful riverside villages. However, a few suggestions of what not to overlook follow:

From Tremolat which is located at the "Cingle de Tremolat", a loop in the path of the river, it is easy to follow the lazy curves of the beautiful Dordogne. When the sun shines you might want to pick out a picnic spot as you drive through a neighboring village of Tremolat, LIMEUIL and consider returning here for lunch or an afternoon rest.   At the juncture of two rivers it is a dear hamlet and has some tables and a very peaceful, grassy setting.

In addition to just driving and absorbing the beauty, a stop should be made at LES EYZIES DE TAYAC.   Referred to as the prehistoric capital, the Cro-Magnon skull was unearthed here.   Installed in the ancient castle of the Barons of Beynac, you might also want to visit its national prehistoric museum. But most impressive are the caves just outside of town at the GROTTO DE FONT DE GAUME.   On the cave walls are incredibly preserved prehistoric drawings. The colors are still so rich that it is hard to comprehend the actual passage of time.   The caves are well worth a visit but the hours are limited and the caves a bit damp and dark.   To avoid disappointment, please reconfirm the hours of visitation.

Boasting one of the loveliest settings, on a wide bend of the Dordogne, the village of BEYNAC ET CAZENAC is a dear town shadowed by its castle.   In the summer months a number of people negotiate the river by boat and Beynac with its wide grassy banks proves to be a popular resting spot. Beynac castle can be reached by climbing directly up the town's narrow streets or by car along a back road.   The furnishings are sparse but the castle is interesting to explore and its dominating position provides some spectacular views of the valley.   Beynac also offers one of the loveliest settings for lunch. On the water's edge the HOTEL BONNET is an excellent choice and it is a memorable treat to dine under vine covered trellises on the riverside terrace. The restaurant-hotel has been operated for generations by the Bonnet family; it easily becomes a highlight of many a trip.

LA ROQUE GAGEAC, a medieval town, appears to climb and cling to the hillside in preference to tumbling into the river.   Very picturesque!   At La Roque there is a grassy area along the river bank with a few picnic tables.

A bit touristy at the height of the season, DOMME is a hilltop village perched on a bend in the Dordogne with views of the valley that remain unchallenged.

Down the river from Domme the CHATEAU DE MONTFORT is definitely worth a visit.   Built by one of the region's most powerful barons, this majestic castle rises out of a rocky ledge. The Chateau de Montfort is not massive and overpowering, but rather, small and intimate.   A private residence, the rooms are elaborately furnished and renovated.

A larger town, SARLAT has an atmospheric old quarter.   Narrow cobbled streets wind through a maze of magnificent gourmet shops and the town square hosts a colorful Saturday morning market.

DAY III   GRAMAT   Chateau de Roumegouse

Travel east along the Dordogne and then south in order to see the Mont Saint Michel of the south, ROCAMADOUR. The road approaching the village is small and twisting but picturesque. Dominated by its church, the city of Rocamadour grips the steep and rugged walls of the Alxon. It is a spectacular site to see and city to visit and has long been a popular pilgrimage spot. (Please note, however that in season it is heavily populated by tourists.)

Not far from Rocamadour is the small town, GRAMAT, possessor of a lovely chateau-hotel. A small sign directed me up a dirt road and through a small village as I searched for this hotel. I was not certain that I had followed the sign correctly until the large majestic tower emerged; peering above the treetops, the CHATEAU DE ROUMEGOUSE revealed itself. A very cordial M Lauwaert, who speaks wonderful English, was the only person at the chateau when I arrived. I wrongly assumed that due to its isolated location, no one knew about it. As it turned out, M Lauwaert had closed a week early that year and I was informed that, to the contrary, even Pompidou and DeGaulle had dined here. Comfortable accommodations will make your stay enjoyable. The dining rooms are elegant with Louis XV furniture. On summer evenings dinner is served on the terrace overlooking the Lot Valley.

DAY IV   VARETZ   Chateau de Castel Novel

The goal today is to reach VARETZ and its hotel CHATEAU DE CASTEL NOVEL. Go ahead and imagine an ideal hotel and the chateau will most likely meet your requirements. It is definitely worth devoting any portion of the day that is left here, enjoying your room, the gracious hospitality, service and mouthwatering food.

After a beautiful winding drive to this magnificent chateau, I was met at my car with smiles and friendly greetings, and my impression was set: Chateau de Castel Novel is a dream! To top it off the cuisine is superb; I never had a more delicious soup than "Veloute de Cepes." There are a relatively small number of rooms. I found, as they were shown, that each one became my "favorite." They are all marvelous, but different. Room #26 lets you sleep in a turret; #19 has a set of magnificent wooden canopied beds; #16, the last room I will mention, has two twin beds, two balconies and a lovely view. I shall return!

When it comes time to depart from this fabulous hotel, travel north to the city of Limoges, justly famous for its porcelain and pottery. A wonderful exposition of ancient and modern ceramics from all over the world is at the national Adrien-Dubonche Museum. From here you can continue to your next destination.

LE LOT

Grotte du Peche-Merle

CABRERETS

MERCUÈS

Conduché

Cahors Bouzies

St Cirq-
Lapopie

Calvignac

La Toulzanie

Carjac

Montbrun

St Pierre-Toirac

Le Lot

Figeac CONQUES

Capdenac

ALTHOUGH LIMITED IN DISTANCE THIS ITINERARY proposes a section of the Lot Valley that travels perhaps the most stunning 51 kilometer stretch in France.   The Lot River Valley rivals the Dordogne and yet remains relatively undiscovered and less traveled.   The road winds along the curves of the wide, calm river, aggressively cutting into the sides of the chalky canyon walls.   At some stretches the route follows the level of the river and at others it straddles the cliff tops.   Vistas are dramatic at every turn, and yet the restricting narrow roads will frustrate the eye of any photographer...there is rarely a place to stop!

DAY I   CAHORS   Chateau de Mercues

Begin at CAHORS a lovely city at the heart of a flourishing wine district.   Of particular interest is the Valentre Bridge with its three impressive towers spanning the River Lot.

Just a few miles from the the city of Cahors is the CHATEAU DE MERCUES perched high on the hills above the Lot River in the small village of Mercues.   For almost twelve centuries the chateau was the base for the Comtes-Eveques of Cahors.   Their names are recorded on plaques in the Chapel. Possession of the Mercues was taken by the State during the revolution. However, in this century the chambers of this magnificent castle are being offered as hotel rooms.   Under new ownership, the Chateau de Mercues maintains its standards as one of France's finest hotels and the chateau alone would warrant a visit to this region.

Most of the luxuriously furnished rooms in the chateau look out through thick castle walls to sweeping vistas of the serene and undeveloped valley. (Note a newly constructed wing of rooms has been added.   They are less expensive and principally built to accommodate seminars and conferences.)

The dining room is outstanding. Elegantly set with the owner's personalized china, the tables are positioned in front of windows that frame the valley through majestic thick stone walls.

The valley is planted with vineyards and Cahor wines are quickly earning an international reputation. I had been impressed by the wines, especially the full-bodied reds, on a previous trip to France, but, as the quantities were limited I was unable to find selections exported to the United States. However, the new owners, the Vigoroux family, are also responsible for some of Cahors finest grapes, and they are now marketing the wines both in New York and California. You can sample them here and savour them again at home with memories of France!

Le Lot

From Cahors the Lot River travels under the Valentre Bridge and begins a path whose beauty remains unchallenged.   The short stretch of river mapped out on this itinerary can be encompassed by car in a day's time, but try to stretch your stay.   This is a region to be roamed at a lazy pace in order to fully appreciate its character and charms.

Each turn presents a new interest.   There are castles, villages whose houses are built into the cliff face, grottos ... glorious scenery! Just two kilometers from the town of CABRERETS, is LA PESCALERIE, the family home of Monsieur Belcour and a spectacular hotel which would do justice to any region. La Pescalerie is a magnificent weathered-stone manor house in a lovely riverside setting in the tranquil Lot Valley.   Ten handsomely appointed bedrooms are divided between two levels and open onto the garden through thick 16th and 17th century walls.   The rooms are pleasingly different, yet each an attractive melange of modern and cherished antiques.   The top floor rooms are set under the beams of the house with delightful dormer windows and a few have lofts ideal for children with a sense of adventure.   The Pescalerie also has a bar and intimate restaurant.   Opened only five years ago, La Pescalerie ideally accommodates those who have the time to linger in the striking Lot Valley.

Set your own pace and simply let the river be your guide.   My stay was sadly limited but Le Lot will be the first destination upon my return to France. Towns and vistas that enchanted me, and that I would like to share with you are as follows:

CABRERETS is a dear village and the nearby GROTTO DU PECH-MERLE is a definite attraction.   Discovered by two fourteen year old boys the vast caverns of this grotto are painted with prehistoric designs (mammoths, bisons, hands, horses) and contain stalagmite columns.

When traveling the road from Cahors, cross the river just before Cabrerets to the village of BOUZIES. Take a moment to look back across the bridge and see the medieval buildings constructed into the walls of the canyon just above the small tunnel. Leaving Bouzies the road climbs and winds to some spectacular vistas of the very picturesque ST CIRQ LAPOPIE. Clinging to sheer canyon walls, this village is a perched cluster of soft ochre and tile roof buildings. St Cirq Lapopie dominates a strategic position on a wide bend of the Lot River and certainly has one of the prettiest settings in the region.

As the river guides you further it proposes a number of lovely towns and with each turn, exposes another angle and view of the Lot valley. LA TOULZANIE is a small village tucked into a bend of the river; pretty and interesting because of the houses built into the hillside. CALVIGNAC is an ancient village, whose fortress clings to a spur on the left bank. On a rocky promintory, the village of MONTBRUN is dressed with the ruins of its fortified castle and looks across to the "SAUT DE LA MOUNINE". Translated roughly as the "Jump of the Monkey", this dramatic cliff face offers incredible views and a legend of romance. It seems to punish his daughter for falling in love with the son of an opposing baron, her father ordered her thrown from the cliffs to her death. Dressed in the clothes of a woman, a monkey fell to its death instead and the sadness and regret that the father felt for his extreme punishment was erased by the joy when he discovered the substitution and that his daughter was still alive. Set on a plateau, the CHATEAU DE LARROQUE-TOIRAC can be visited and presents an impressive silhouette against the chalky cliffs and the town of ST PIERRE TOIRAC.

DAY III   CONQUES   Hotel Ste Foy

CONQUES is a bonus to this itinerary but requires that you journey a short distance beyond the Lot River. Unfortunately, after FIGEAC the idyllic scenery of the Lot valley is interrupted by larger cities and traffic. But quiet prevails once again as you detour up a narrow river canyon in the direction of Conques.

The medieval village of Conques has a dramatic position overlooking the Doudon Canyon. Tucked a considerable distance off the beaten track, it is a delightful, unspoilt village to explore - especially glorious in the gentle light of evening or in the misty fog of early day. Conques' pride is a classic 13th century church. Directly across from the church, is a simple, but charming hotel, the STE FOY. Some of the shuttered windows of the rooms open onto the quiet cobbled village streets, others open onto the hotel's inner courtyard or up to the church steeples. Wake in the morning to the melodious church bells that warm the silence of the village and ring out to the surrounding hills. The decor of the Ste Foy is neat and attractive and one can't improve upon its location. Dinner is served family style on a sheltered courtyard terrace. The menu offers a number of regional specialties and is very reasonable in price. The hotel's finest feature is Madame Canne. Her charm, welcoming smile and attitude to please create the wonderful atmosphere of the Ste Foy. It is easy to settle happily here and Conques serves as a delightful conclusion to this itinerary.

Le Lot

BASQUE

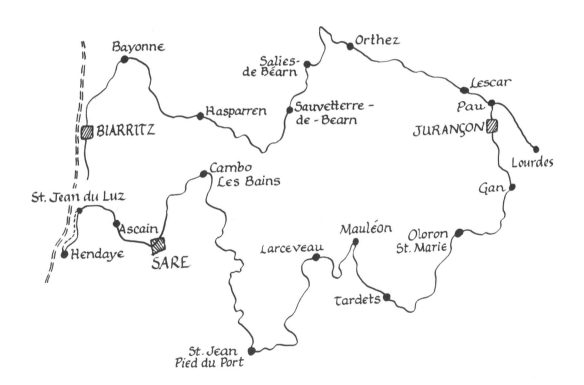

Bayonne

Orthez

Salies-
de Béarn

Lescar

Hasparren

Sauveterre -
de - Bearn

Pau

BIARRITZ

JURANÇON

Lourdes

Cambo
Les Bains

Gan

St. Jean du Luz

Ascain

Mauléon

Oloron
St. Marie

Larceveau

Hendaye

SARE

Tardets

St. Jean
Pied du Port

THIS ITINERARY TRACES A PATH THROUGH A REGION of France that has guarded more of its character than any other. There are seven Basque provinces; three in France: Labourd, Basse and Navarre, and four in Spain: Biscaye, Guipuzcoa, Navarre and Alava. Concerning the seven there is a saying: "Zaspiak-bet", which means "seven equals one". The race, language called Euskara and the style of life are similar throughout the region. The Pays Basque geographically marks the end of the Pyrenees mountains. Starting from the coast, the region is abundant in beautiful landscapes, sandy stretches of beach, beautiful valleys sliced by winding rivers, rolling green hills, forests, grottos, canyons and its own mountain range. The Basque add additional contrasts to the colorful region, and their houses, scattered or in small clusters, dot the countryside. The most charming are the white homes with red roofs called the Labourdine. The houses of Basse and Navarre are of stone and have circular balconies, and in Soule they are characterized by pointed slate roofs. The Basque themselves often wear their traditional costumes, never without a beret.

DAY I: SARE   Hotel Arraya

HENDAYE is the last town before the border and more Spanish in character than French. Drive north along the corniche and with each turn the road presents stunning views of the coast and stretches of sandy beach. ST JEAN DE LUZ is a charming port town. Clustered on small streets and squares its shops and restaurants cater to a number of travelers attracted by the area's expanse of beaches. It is typically Basque in appearance with its harbor filled with red and blue fishing boats piled high with nets and dozens of fishermen proudly sorting and evaluating their catches.

Travel from the coast and venture out along the Route des Pyrenees. The drive takes you through quaint villages and leaves you with a wonderful impression of the region. The blend of the French and Spanish cultures and scenery is perfect.

Basque is a captivating region, especially in late summer at festival time. There are folklore dances, song and game shows to attend and the original jai alai, native of Basque to observe. The small town of SARE, set in the Basque hills just a few miles from the coast captivated me on a morning in August. Local boys dressed in starched white uniforms, accented by red ties and berets led a procession to Church. The women shuttled the immaculately clothed children into the church while the local elder men ignored the fanfare and stood outside discussing the politics of the world, (if not their little village), until they were summoned by the church bells. It was a local holiday and it seemed to typify the patriotism of the region.

The HOTEL ARRAYA sits on the the town's main square and a local girl attracted me to its outdoor patio-restaurant with her delicious gateau basque and her smile. The hotel, a former wayside inn on the pilgrimage road to Santiago de Compostela is decorated in the style of the finest Basque residences of the 17th century. The entry, lobby and breakfast nook are dressed with charm. Cozy blue and white gingham cushions pad the wooden chairs that sit round a beautiful collection of antique tables. The restaurant offers regional specialities and one must stay here long enough to sample them all. The Hotel Arraya is managed by Paul Fagoaga and he is present to welcome his guests as friends, "Zizilua".

DAY II   PAU (JURANCON)   Hotel du Canastel

From Sare the road continues through farmland and soon arrives at the inland resort of CAMBO LES BAINS. This dear town is composed largely of villas and hotels overlooking the Nive Valley. The old Basque village is nestled along the river banks.

From Cambo les Bains the road begins to wind, and as the countryside gains altitude, the pastures remain, but valleys, deep rivers and the snow-capped Pyrenees are added to the scene. The colors are unbelievable. Hillsides are a palette of reds, golds, oranges yellows and greens.

Situated at the foot of the pass crossing the Spanish border, ST JEAN PIED DE PORT on the River Nive is the next destination. It was once the capital of Basse Navarre. Continuing east on the route of the Pyrenees you will shortly pass through Col d'Osquich, a high point. A few miles further still is the town of MAULEON SOULE. A feudal village, it is also an important shoe-making center. You might want to take time to search out a small shop whose entrance is shaded by hat stands, and an imaginative old woman whose constant smile cojoles someone into buying one of her berets - one whose size and color suits him, of course!

TARDETS, a charming town, is the folklore center of the Soule province. A sign on the outskirts describes it as the "mirror of the Basque country." Between Tardets and Oloron Ste. Marie, as the road climbs, is a small, lovely village, MONTORY.   At the foot of the Pyrenees gray with snow, it sits upon a carpet of contrasting green.   OLORON STE MARIE is an industrial center, yet it does have a charming old quarter and medieval church.

After your day of dazzling beauty, I suggest you stop in Jurancon where you can enjoy a delicious evening meal and a delightful rest at the HOTEL DU CANASTEL.   Hotel Du Canastel is just off the main road to Pau.   Ideal for the hot summer months, it has a lovely pool bordered by a patio and enclosed by greenery.   There are twelve attractive rooms, all with bath.   Four of the rooms are in an annex and open directly onto the pool area.   In the main building, the "rose" room (double) and the "blue" room (twins) overlook the pool.   The restaurant is more than adequate with a large selection of grilled fish, lobster, shrimp and roasts smothered in delicious sauces.

It is only a few miles north from Jurancon to the city of PAU, where you find a panoramic view of the Pyrenees. Also of interest is the 12th century chateau, the birthplace of Louis IV, the Eighteenth Century Palace of Navarre and the Tour de la Monnaie (a mint). From Pau it is a convenient detour to the pilgrimage spot of LOURDES before commencing a return drive to the coast.

An overwhelming number of tourist shops capitalize on the droves of people attracted to the very moving and mystifying pilgrimage spot of Lourdes. But, once on the grassy stretches below the cathedral, the rushing water blocks out the distracting noises of the busy city streets. A constant parade of patients, ushered in on stretchers and in wheel chairs, seek the miracle cures that the religious history of Lourdes promises. I was overwhelmed by both the range in ages and numbers of people, crippled and ill, and by the the sadness and hope seen in the eyes of those who accompany them. To experience Lourdes is very emotional and moving.

LESCAR, not far from Pau, has an ancient Roman Cathedral and was Bearn's first capital.

ORTHEZ, a lively village where much of the famous Bayonne ham is produced, has an old fortified bridge as it main attraction. SALIES DE BEARN is a popular spa resort in a pleasant location. Sauveterre is another town occupying a lovely, picturesque spot. At OXOCELLHAYA et ISTURITS there are grottos. After HASPARREN, the drive and views are beautiful all the way to BAYONNE. A few unhurried hours should be reserved to explore the colorful city of Bayonne.

BIARRITZ affords a lingering sample of the taste, style and life of the Pays Basque. It was once a simple fishing village now recognized as a seaside resort attracting celebrities year round. For your first destination there is a fabulous hotel found on the outskirts of Biarritz.

CHATEAU DE BRINDOS resembles a Spanish chateau appropriately located in the Basque country. The hotel is magnificently situated on the Lac de Brindos. It has its own dock with ducks and swans adding to the romantic setting. The entry, grand salon and dining rooms are very impressive with their medieval architecture. Of the twenty luxurious bedrooms, I particularly liked #17, a corner room with a beautiful canopied four-poster facing the lake, and #11, a large room with twin beds and a quaint round salon, all decorated in gold. The gastronomic restaurant offers such selections as "mille feuilles de jambon" and "fruite souffle au champagne."

Basque

GORGES du TARN

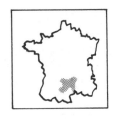

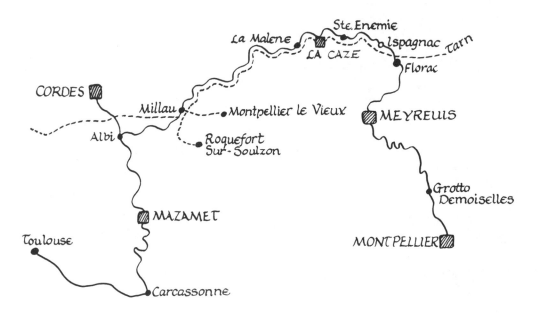

Ste. Enemie
La Malène
Ispagnac
LA CAZE
Tarn
Florac
CORDES
Millau
Montpellier le Vieux
MEYREUIS
Albi
Roquefort
Sur-Soulzon
Grotto
Demoiselles
MAZAMET
Toulouse
MONTPELLIER
Carcassonne

THE TARN CANYON IS TRULY SPECTACULAR. This itinerary follows the Tarn River as it winds back and forth along the canyon. With each turn the drive becomes that much more beautiful, never monotonous. I discovered the canyon in early autumn and I am now convinced it is the perfect time to plan a visit. I had all the beauty to myself. The French were back at work or in school and the narrow mountain road (which if crowded might be dangerous) was deserted. The grass carpeting the mountains and hillsides was lush, all shades of green, and the trees blazed gold, red and orange in the sunlight. I drove, hiked and picnicked my way through the Tarn Canyon and loved every moment. It is also possible to take a 1-1/4 hour boat trip that originates at La Malene and costs approximately 100 Francs including a return taxi trip.

This itinerary begins at Montpellier, follows the canyon of the Tarn, includes a visit to the walled city of Carcassonne and finishes in the city of Toulouse.

DAY I   MONTPELLIER   Demeure de Brousses

MONTPELLIER, a university town since the 17th century, can be considered the "Oxford" and "Cambridge" of France. The pace is lively and happy. It is a perfect town for window shopping or sipping coffee on the Place de la Comedie.

At night, if you want to leave the noise behind, the DEMEURE DES BROUSSES is everything you could wish for. On the outskirts of Montpellier, this is a marvelous old chateau removed from the noise and tension of the city. Spacious and grand, the manor is beautifully furnished and has a cozy, inviting sitting room. The rooms are all with bath and are lovely. Room #16 is the most expensive, but also the nicest, with its own balcony and splendid views. The restaurant, in a neighboring building, is known for the quality of its food. The receptionist spoke wonderful English.

DAY II   MEYREUIS   Chateau D'Ayres

It would be best not to dawdle but to get off to an early start today in order that you may enjoy the drive at your leisure. From Montpellier travel approximately thirty miles to the famous "GROTTO DES DEMOISELLES." Discovered in 1770, it is perhaps the best grotto of all to visit.

From here it is a lovely drive to MEYREUIS and tonight's hotel. Overpowered by the towering Jonte Canyon Walls, the picturesque buildings of Meyreuis huddle together along the banks of the Jonte. A farm road's distance from this quaint village is the enchanting CHATEAU D'AYRES. Hidden behind a high stone wall, this superb hotel has managed to preserve and protect its special atmosphere, beauty and peacefulness.

The chateau was built in the 12th century as a Benedictine monastery. In its past the chateau has been burned, rampaged and owned by an ancestor of the Rockefellers, DeNogart, the man charged with stopping Pope Benedictine VIII at Anangi. It was purchased by the present family when the senior Monsieur Teyssier du Cros came to ask for the hand of his love and recognized the grounds as where he had played as a child. The Teyssier du Cros family operated the Chateau d'Ayres for a number of years until they sold it in the late 1970s to a young and enthusiastic couple, Jean Francois and Chantal de Monthou. It is under their care and devotion that the hotel is managed today. Now there are twenty-two beautiful bedchambers instead of the original two. Works of culinary art are created in the kitchen daily.

The Chateau d'Ayres, which has a character formed by so many events and personalities, is a lovely and attractive hotel and will definitely put you in an ideal mood to start out tomorrow on an excursion into the Tarn Canyon.

This morning drive northeast to the town of FLORAC, the starting point of the canyon.   From Florac continue north in the direction of Mende but at the town of Biesset head west.   The Ispagnac Basin, located at the entrance to the canyon, is filled with fruit trees, vineyards and strawberries.   Here towns are scattered artistically about; chateaux and ruins appear often enough to add enchantment.   SAINTE ENIMIE is a pretty town caught in the bend of the canyon.   An old attractive bridge arches across the river and a church wedged into the mountain side piques the curiousity.

A surprise is in store for you just a short distance south of STE ENIMIE, where majestically positioned above the Tarn is a fairy tale castle.   You will be excited to know that this marvelous castle, CHATEAU DE LA CAZE, is also your hotel.   Here you can settle for a few days and at your own pace and fancy explore the Gorges du Tarn.   There are many quaint towns to visit: LA MALENE, LES VIGNES, LA MUSE (HOTEL DE LA MUSE has a superb restaurant with a panoramic view), POINT SUBLIME.   Then, at the end of each day, you can return to your own castle and be royally taken care of by Madame Roux.   Although each room at the chateau is like a king's bedchamber, room #6 is the most beautiful of all.   It has a large wooden canopied bed and an entire wall of windows overlooking the Tarn and canyon.   It was the apartment of Sonbeyrane Alamand, a niece of the Prior Francois Alamand.   She chose the location and had the chateau built in 1489 to serve as her honeymoon haven.   There are paintings on the ceiling of the eight sisters who later inherited the chateau. These eight sisters, according to legend, were very beautiful and had secret rendezvous each night with their lovers in the castle garden.

The restaurant in the chateau has several house specialities; for dinner you might choose "caneton chateau de la caze" or "les filets de fruit sombeyrane."

DAY IV   CORDES   Hotel Grand Ecuyer

When you eventually do decide to leave the Tarn Canyon and the Chateau de la Caze, the drive scheduled will demand an early start.   The only negative is that MILLAU sadly marks the end of the canyon.   The agreeable city is known for its leather goods, particularly gloves.   MONTPELLIER LE VIEUX is an intriguing rock formation northeast of Millau and southeast is the city responsible for the distinctive roquefort cheese, Roquefort sur Solzon.   If this regional speciality appeals, you might enjoy a tour of one of the cheese cellars.
        ALBI is about a two-hour drive through farmland from Roquefort. Mostly brick with its cathedral dominating the entire city, Albi is also referred

to as "Albi the red." The Toulouse Lautrec Museum is one of its more interesting attractions.

Another half hour drive and the last destination for today is reached. A perched village, watching over the Cerou Valley, CORDES has been given the poetic title of "Cordes in the heavens." Known for its leather goods and handwoven fabrics, the city offers many shops to explore along its cobble-stoned streets.

Found in the heart of this medieval city is the HOTEL DU GRAND ECUYER, a choice spot to spend the night. It is filled with antiques and charm from the ground entrance to the slanting upper levels. The rooms are impressive with their large old beds, often a fireplace and magnificent views of the velvet green valley below. The hotel has a good restaurant and attractive bar.

Scheduled for today is a simple drive south to PONT DE L'ARN and your hotel this evening, CHATEAU DE MONTLEDIER, which is tucked into the beauty and quiet of the Black Mountains.   There is plenty of time to sleep or to return to that "atelier" in Cordes and contemplate once more whether to purchase that woven blanket or to revisit the city of Albi.   But no matter how you spend your day, waiting for you at its end will be a delicious meal and a romantic bedroom.

Once you have arrived at the chateau and developed a taste for the splendor and elegance it offers, you will never want to leave but when you do, you will never forget the route back. The seven rooms are magnificent; Raymond, in my opinion, is the loveliest of all, with two stunning antique canopied beds and a spacious, modern bathroom. The restaurant in the cellar is quite intimate. The cuisine is marvelous and the service impressive; everything is done to perfection and with taste. This is one place where the specialities outnumber the rooms - "cote de boeuf girestiere" is super!

Located just a few miles south of Pont de l'Arn is CARCASSONE, Europe's largest medieval fortress and a highlight of this itinerary. Carcassone rises above the vineyards at the foot of the Cevennes and Pyrenees. The massive walls protecting the town were first raised by the Romans in the First Century B.C. Never conquered in battle, the mighty city lost to the elements but has been restored. It looks as it did when constructed centuries ago. One glimpse back at the city with its impressive towers and walls will send you wandering back into history as you drive towards TOULOUSE, always in a pink glow. In the midst of a rich agricultural district, 'France's 4th city' has become a very important industrial center with electronics and aerospace research as principal interests. It is also a large artistic center plus has many sights worth seeing such as Church Basilique St. Sermin, old homes and various museums.

Here your journey ends.

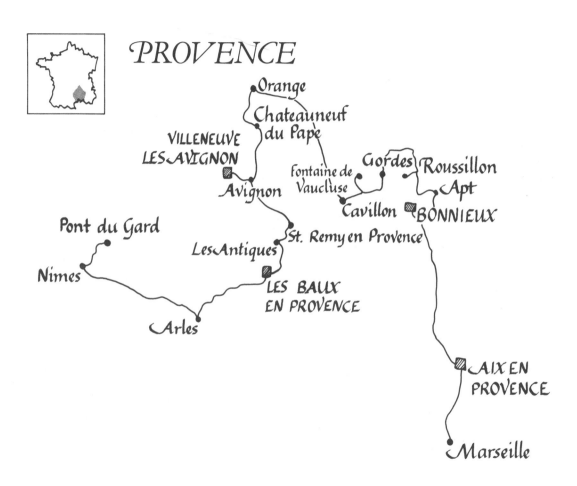

PROVENCE

Orange

Chateauneuf
du Pape

VILLENEUVE
LES AVIGNON

Fontaine de
Vaucluse

Gordes

Roussillon

Apt

Avignon

Cavillon

BONNIEUX

Pont du Gard

Les Antiques

St. Remy en Provence

Nimes

LES BAUX
EN PROVENCE

Arles

AIX EN
PROVENCE

Marseille

PROVENCE, SETTLED BY THE ROMANS AROUND 120 B.C., is a region of contrasts and colors. Also known as the "Midi", it is associated with a mild climate, friendly smiles and a warm welcome.

DAY I   AIX EN PROVENCE   Hotel Le Pigonnet

MARSEILLES is the second largest city in France according to population. Settled as a Phoenician colony, this major Mediterranean port has twenty-five centuries of history and is where this tour of Provence begins. Apart from the Roman docks and fortified church of Saint Victor, there are few monuments within the city to its past. However, you must see La Canabiere, a major boulevard which captures the activity, gaiety and pace of Marseilles. The old port offers a number of museums to draw your interest; the Grobet-Labadie Museum has a beautiful collection of tapestries, furniture, paintings, musical instruments, pottery and sculpture.

From Marseilles drive north to AIX EN PROVENCE. It is a cheerful city and deserves time to be properly visited. It was once the capital of Provence and also a great art center in the time of King Rene. There are a number of impressive fountains, hidden squares, charming little back streets lined with shops, and majestic avenues. The beckoning cobble-stone streets of the old quarter are intriguing to wander at night and the illuminated tree-lined Boulevard Mirabeau is enchanting ... a bit reminiscent of Paris with its many sidewalk cafes. From the fountain it is just a fifteen minute walk to the very professionally run and attractive HOTEL LE PIGONNET. A road shaded by trees leads you to this hotel away from the noise and traffic of the city. Here you will find an abundance of flowers, cozy sitting rooms, a heated swimming pool, a fine restaurant and pleasant bedrooms.

While in Aix en Provence, with Le Pigonnet as your base, and weather permitting, you can stroll down the old streets or join the crowd having coffee in one of the many cafes on the Boulevard Mirabeau. Nineteen 17th century tapestries from Beauvois are on display in the Museum of Tapestries. Another fifteen Flemish tapestries can be found in the Cathedral Saint Sauveur. Aix is also where Paul Cezanne studied with Emile Zola, and traces of his past can be seen throughout the city.

DAY II   BONNIEUX   Le Prieure

From Aix travel north on country roads through groves of olive trees and acres of vineyards to the hilltowns of Provence. Less traveled, the medieval perched villages of this region are delightful and intriguing to explore. BONNIEUX is a charming town. Guarding a picturesque setting on a plateau above the Luberon Valley, Bonnieux affords a most convenient location to settle as well as

accommodations at one of France's loveliest hotels. LE PRIEURE is absolutely charming because of the owner and the enchanting decor of the inn. I was surprised to discover a hotel of such superior quality tucked away in this small hillside village until I learned that the owner, Monsieur Chapotin is a member of a family long responsible for some of France's finest and most prestigious hotels. Having recently left a career of finance behind in Paris, Monsieur Chapotin has chosen this small 17th century catholic abbey as his new venture and second home. You will discover incredible antiques in a setting of luxurious calm. Le Prieure has a superb restaurant with specialities all too impossible to resist. A list to tempt even the most disciplined: Foe gras frais de canard; Canard aux olives de Nyon; Saumon a l'oiselle; Truite marinee au vinaigre; Gateau au chocolat! The restaurant is a gorgeous place to linger in the evening. It is decorated with soft, pale pink table cloths, fresh flowers, soft lighting. On warmer evenings meals are served in the shade of the garden.

The traditionally beautiful bedrooms are excellent in the choice and enhancement of decor. It is hard not to take special notice of the magnificent pieces of art and paintings found throughout the inn. Monsieur Chapotin has a definite appreciation for art and has plans to turn the adjoining chapel into a gallery.

Under the care and direction of Monsieur Chapotin and Charlotte Keller, Le Prieure is outstanding and will most certainly enhance your travels in Provence!

To include in your explorations are the two neighboring towns of ROUSSILLON and GORDES. Roussillon is a maze of narrow streets and small shops and restaurants that climb to the town's summit. In various shades of ochres Roussillon is a particularly pretty city, especially on a clear day when the sun warms and intensifies the colors. Gordes, a perched village marking an end to the Vaucluse plateaux and dominating the Imergue Valley is dressed in tones of gray and is a wonderful town to explore.

Known for its surrounding fields responsible for the delicious melons, CAVILLON is another village to include should your schedule permit. From Cavillon continue north to the amazing FOUNTAIN DE VAUCLUSE. In the late afternoon as the sun begins its descent, walk around the celebrated natural fountain. Quite striking, at certain times of the year the shooting water is so powerful that it becomes dangerous and the fountain is closed to observers. The most dramatic seasons to visit are either winter or spring.

DAY III   VILLENEUVE LES AVIGNON   Le Prieure

From Bonnieux point yourself in the direction of ORANGE. The drive is an easy one and takes approximately an hour and a half. The people I encountered in Orange were helpful and friendly. The city has character, and the antique theater and commemorative arch, improperly named the "Arc de Triomphe", are worth seeing.

Just south of the city travel the wine road of some of the world's most treasured labels. The grapes of CHATEAUNEUF DU PAPE were first planted to fill the reserve of the Papal city of Avignon. Watch for the signs to the chateau. Although it has been in ruins since the religious wars, its skeleton still secures a fabulous hilltop position and offers sweeping views of the region. The chateau would serve as a spectacular picnic spot or for a more elaborate feast consider the excellent dining room of the HOSTELLERIE FINES ROCHES. It seems only appropriate that in an area responsible for some of the finest wines is also the location for an outstanding restaurant-hotel. Monsieur Estevenin is a gracious host to some very famous clientele and although he still oversees the kitchen, his son is now in charge as the chef. The Hostellerie Fines Roches is just off the wine route and its turrets are easy to spot.

In the 14th century AVIGNON was the seat of the Papacy. The Palace of the Popes is grand and dwarfs the rest of the city. Devote the majority of your time to visiting the feudal structure, but if you have time to spare, journey out to the Pont Saint Benezet, constructed with pedestrians and horsemen in mind, and to the Calvet Museum which has a rich collection of artifacts and paintings from the School of Avignon. A walled city, Avignon remains one of the most interesting and beautiful of the medieval cities of Europe.

VILLENEUVE LES AVIGNON is separated from Avignon by the Rhone River. It is a stronghold which has retained several military buildings including the Philippe le Bel Tower, where the caretaker will tell you all the historic facts he feels you lack, and the Fort Saint Andre. Following the good advice of some Sunday strollers, I hiked up to the fort and enjoyed the view I found across the Rhone to Avignon and the Popes' Palace.

Villeneuve's treasures have not all been mentioned yet. There is a 13th century priory awaiting you. It was constructed by order of Cardinal Arnaud de Via and was purchased and transformed into a first-class hotel in 1943 by M Mille. The rooms of LE PRIEURE are bursting at the seams with charm. Be sure to take advantage of the beautiful pool and lovely gardens.

DAY IV   LES BAUX EN PROVENCE   L'Oustau Baumaniere

From Avignon it is a very pleasant drive south along a lazy, tree-lined road to ST REMY EN PROVENCE.   Of interest is the priory where Van Gogh was nursed, a Romanesque church, Renaissance houses and a busy public square.   Just a mile or so on the outskirts of town are LES ANTIQUES.   This is the site of the excavations of an ancient Glanum: an arch and a mausoleum, both pretty much intact.

          The final destination for today is LES BAUX EN PROVENCE in the Alpilles just a few miles southeast of St Remy.   This city derives it name from Bauxite, the mineral discovered there, and is interesting to explore, as it has retained its heroic and Provencal charm.   The ruins appear to be a continuation of the rocky spur from which they rise.   There are a number of craft shops and inviting creperies tucked away. From Les Baux you will not only have splendid views of the area but you will have a sneak preview of your marvelous hotel for tonight, nestled down below.

L'OUSTAU BAUMANIERE is full of wonderful surprises and is also where the action takes place in Alistair MacLean's novel, *Caravan to Vacarres*. Set among flowers, trees and gardens, the hotel has a lovely pool, the best food in Provence and bedrooms and service that deserve only praise. Ask your waiter to suggest some of the house specialities if you find it impossible to limit your selection after studying the menu.

DAY V   NIMES   Hotel Imperator

The distance to be covered today is relatively short but the sites to be seen are very important. ARLES is a city abounding in character, a truly lovely city whose growth was governed by the banks and curves of the Rhone River. It is a

Roman-influenced port city, glorified because of its magnificent Gallo-Roman arenas and theaters. Arles is a city too valuable and rewarding to omit.

NIMES lies approximately only twenty miles west of Arles. A Gallic capital, it was also popular with the Romans who built its monuments. Without fail you should see the amphitheater that once held 21,000 spectators, the arenas, Maison Carre, (one of the best preserved temples), and the magnificent fountain gardens. I would suggest taking in both the sunrise and the sunset as they highlight the monuments.

Nimes is a fun, lively city and the HOTEL IMPERATOR gives you the chance to stay here a while longer. Located across from the park it manages to find some peace and quiet in the middle of Nimes. All the rooms are with either shower or bath. Each is spacious and decorated with antiques and those facing the garden are only eleven francs more. Some rooms have balconies at no extra cost, so you definitely should make a point of asking for one.

The spectacular Pont du Gard is just twelve miles or so north of Nimes. Still intact, it dates back two thousand years and will remain one of the world's marvels.   It served as an aquaduct controlling the flow of mineral waters from Uzes to Nimes.   The bridge straddles the Rhone, towering more than 120 feet; it is awe-inspiring.

Depending on your time schedule, you might want to leave your luggage one more day at the Hotel Imperator and take a short trip south from Nimes to the 13th century walled city of AIGUES MORTES. It is surrounded by the CAMARGUE, a region of marshland romanticized by the presense of its wild horses and gypsies.

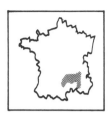

GORGES
du VERDON

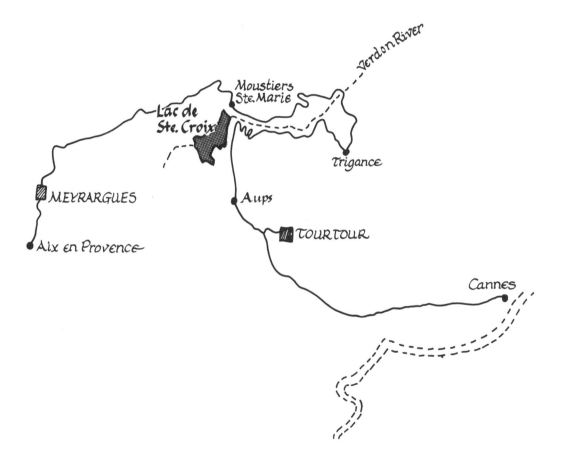

THE GORGES DU VERDON IS THE FRENCH equivalent of the Grand Canyon, but with an even greater variety of colors.   The Verdon River, a tributary of the Durance, flows past the plateaux rich in lime, through the magnificent canyons of the Haute Provence, and then plunges into the dramatic trench-like Gorges du Verdon enclosed with jagged walls of mountains.   The area is convenient to visit when traveling from the Cote d'Azur toward central Provence; a few days spent in this region will prove memorable.

DAY I   TOURTOUR   Bastide de la Tourtour

Departing early from cosmopolitan Cannes you can either take the coastal route, a bit more demanding in time or the autoroute through the mountains in the direction of Aix en Provence.   The coastal route sets off in the direction of Saint Raphael.   The coastline between La Napoule and Saint Raphael is rugged and has been called the "CORNICHE D'OR" (golden mountain road).   The road is a chain of spectacular views: everywhere the fire red mountains contrast dramatically with the dark blue sea.   SAINT RAPHAEL is a small commercial port with a pleasant beach frequented by tourists throughout the year.   Leaving Saint Raphael the road leads towards SAINT TROPEZ along the MASSIF DES MAURES.   En route are dozens of small ports and beaches.   But Saint Tropez, an active port where each fisherman sorts and displays his catch, is easily the most enchanting of all.

Drive inland at Ste Maxime along a scenic mountain road that connects with N7 at LE MUY.   Cross the N7 and continue north in the direction of DRAGUIGNAN and watch for signs to TOURTOUR.   The drive is beautiful, along a quiet country road weaving between mountains, through vineyards and among the French.   It is wonderful; I drove for hours and never passed a single car.   The BASTIDE DE LA TOURTOUR is a marvelous hotel located on the outskirts and is actually higher than the town of Tourtour, the "city in the heavens."

The provincial-styled rooms all have a bath and twelve have terraces. Being on top of the world, or at least of Provence, you have panoramic views of the region. From the swimming pool area or in the grand restaurant you can relax and watch the evening fall on the valley below. The chef prepares divine cuisine, and there is an outdoor grill for summer. Sample the house treats- "loup a l'oseille" or "tournedos aux truffes." The Bastide has a very pleasant and friendly atmosphere.

Gorges du Verdon

It is best to begin with an early departure today so that it will be possible to tour the Verdon Canyon at leisure.   Traveling both roads encircling it, you are able to view every aspect and angle of the impressive canyon.

North of AUPS on D957, the road soon connects with D19, the south bank or CORNICHE SUBLIME. Along this drive of about two hours, the most startling and magnificent views are exposed. Just past LA COURNERELLE head north towards LA TRIGANCE, a convenient half-way point. The chateau here is a wonderful place to stop for lunch, if you have not already packed a picnic. The cellar restaurant of CHATEAU DE LA TRIGANCE and its delicacies have attracted gourmets from all over France.

Continue now on D955 winding through the valley and at PONT DE SOLEILS pass once again through the jagged mouth of the Verdon Canyon. Every second the drive is spectacular. The canyon is almost overpowering. Its sides plunge down to depths far below where dark, blue-green pools reflect the rushing river. The road veers away from the edge at points and rolls past beautiful green meadows dotted by a few mountain cabins and small villages. There are many ideal picnic spots, so many that it will be difficult to choose one. Wild flowers bloom everywhere. Descriptions pale beside the beauty of the region. The road gradually returns to the valley, and at the end is the quaint village of MOUSTIERS STE MARIE, famous for its pottery.

Leaving the canyon behind, drive towards MEYRARGUES, a small town approximately 15 miles from Aix en Provence. A small road winds up from the tiny town to tonight's hotel, the CHATEAU DE MEYRARGUES, which dominates the village. It was in 1952 that the chateau became a hotel. Once the stronghold for the mightiest lords of Provence, it is still today majestic and fit for nobility. The building, in the shape of a U, shelters a peaceful terrace where you can enjoy a delicious breakfast and see for miles. All of the rooms are beautiful, some truly exceptional: "Napoleon" with a large canopy and red velvet curtains tied to each corner, appears unchanged from the day the titled inhabitants departed. The cuisine is first rate.

Tomorrow continue to AIX EN PROVENCE, where you can connect with other transportation if you wish.

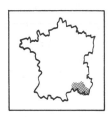

CÔTE d'AZUR

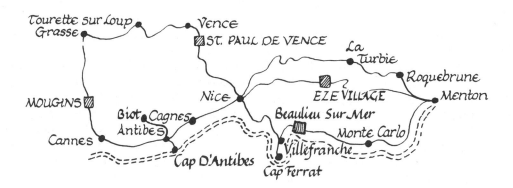

Tourette sur Loup
Grasse
Vence
ST. PAUL DE VENCE
La Turbie
Roquebrune
MOUGINS
Nice
EZE VILLAGE
Menton
Biot Cagnes
Beaulieu Sur Mer
Antibes
Monte Carlo
Cannes
Cap D'Antibes
Villefranche
Cap Ferrat

THE COTE D'AZUR IS KNOWN FOR ITS CONTINUOUS stretch of beaches, clear blue water, sunshine and the habits of the wealthy who made it infamous. Now filled with millions of tourists, or rather sun-worshippers, the coastal cities are always bustling, active and guarantee excitement. In the mountains overlooking the Mediterranean are a number of smaller, "perched" villages, removed from the continuous activity of the Cote and offering a beautiful, peaceful setting.

DAY I   ST PAUL DE VENCE   La Colombe D'Or

The French Riviera or the Cote d'Azur actually is the area between Menton and Nice. Even the French say the "Nicoise" are not typically French, they are more gentle and agreeable. Our tour begins at its capital, NICE, "Queen of the Riviera". Nice is colorful, elegant and always a bustle of activity. Nice is a large city with an old section and a new section. The old town is quite colorful with its flower market and magnificent Baroque churches. The Promenade des Anglais, a contrast, runs along the seashore, and is lined with elegant hotels and casinos. Lighted at night, it is a wonderful place to stroll.

Having only just arrived on the Cote d'Azur you will probably be eager to settle down and rest. I know that once you arrive at LA COLOMBE D'OR, located opposite the main square on the gates to the fortified town of ST. PAUL DE VENCE, you will be thankful that you did check in early, for here you will savor every minute. The hotel has many attractive salons, a refreshing pool and rustic rooms. The restaurant of La Colombe D'Or is both excellent and attractive. Dine either in the intimacy of a room warmed by a cozy fire or on the patio underneath the shade of grape vines. The hotel boasts a fantastic collection of art. In the past a number of now famous painters paid for their meals with their talents .. and the reputation of the inn dictates that one compliments the other!

Settle in your room and then stop for a drink at the outdoor terrace-bar of the neighboring Cafe de la Paix.   It is an ideal place to relax and you will be entertained by the locals playing "boules".   The town of St. Paul de Vence is a picturesque mountain village.   Fortified, it once guarded the ancient Var Frontier.   Cars are forbidden inside the old city and so it is necessary to go on foot beyond the ramparts to enjoy the feudal world of this perched town.   The town is a cluster of galleries and tourist shops, cobbled streets and walls from which there are panoramic views of the ever-expanding hilltowns of the Riviera.

Just outside of town is the MAEGHT FOUNDATION.   This is a private museum that sponsors and hosts numerous collections of some of the world's finest contemporary artists.

Just a short distance north of St. Paul de Vence is another mountain town, VENCE. Here, there are dozens of back streets with interesting shops to discover and delicious pastries to sample. Leave Vence in the direction of Grasse along the small mountain road I adore. If I had only a bicycle with me I would have loved to join the many enthusiasts I passed, all taking advantage of the lovely weather and quiet shady roads.

On the way to Grasse you will pass through a few more towns. Each consists of a cluster of medieval buildings and winding, narrow streets that, without exception, encircle a towering church and its steeple. TOURETTES SUR LOUP is just one of the perched towns you will see. After the Second World War it became active again in the textile market as it had been in the Middle Ages. Now it is one of the top "tissage a main" centers in the world. The workshops and stores are open to the public and fascinating to visit.

Road signs will not be necessary. You will know by the sweet fragrance of flowers when you have arrived in the perfume center of GRASSE. The city is constantly growing but the old section is fun to wander through, a tour of one of the factories-Fragonard or Molinard-is interesting and the views of the valley below are breathtaking.

This region of roses, oeillets, violettes, jasmine, olives and oranges is too enchanting to hurry through so why not explore the fortified town of MOUGINS, only seven miles south of Grasse. It is characteristic of many of the medieval villages and can only be seen on foot, which luckily preserves the atmosphere that horns and motors all too often obliterate. Located in the center of Mougins is a small courtyard decorated with a fountain and flowers and shaded by trees. Here you will discover a few small cafes where local inhabitants meet to gossip about Society, Life and Politics.

On the outskirts of Mougins in the direction of Cannes is a marvelous inn, LE MOULIN DE MOUGINS. It is actually a 16th century mill, and once off the busy road to Cannes one enjoys a beautiful and calm setting. At the same time it is only a few miles from the activity at the Cote d'Azur, which gives you an opportunity to escape from or to return to it, whichever you prefer.

Each of the rooms is charming and comfortable, and the personal attention you will receive during your stay will amaze you. I was followed and helped by so many people that I kept bumping into them. The cuisine is prepared by the owner himself, Mr. Roger Verge, and is superb. All of his courses are universally known, particularly his "pate de sole", "encroute sauce grilott" and his "supreme de loup auguste escoffier". From now, whenever I hear the name Le Moulin de Mougins, I will recall the charm of this small inn and the promise I made to myself to return there some day soon.

Cote D'Azur

If you have not used up your entire vacation enjoying and pampering yourself at Le Moulin de Mougins, you may now continue south, returning to the coast and the enchanting, cosmopolitan city of CANNES.   On the Golfe de Napoule, Cannes is the center for many festivals, most famous being the Cannes Film Festival, held annually in May.   The Boulevard de la Croissette is a wide street bordered by palm trees separating the beach and the large new hotels and apartment buildings.   Le Suquet quarter at the west end of the popular boulevard is from the past and has a superior view of the colorful port.

You might also be interested in taking an excursion from Cannes to the LERINS ISLANDS where you can look back and enjoy a splendid view of the coast.   On the ISLAND OF SAINTE MARGUERITE it is exciting to visit the prison which held Scott's Man in the Iron Mask, and on the ISLAND OF SAINT HONORAT there is a fortified monastery to investigate.

Around the bend from Cannes, returning in the direction of Nice approximately seven miles, is the small elite town of CAP D'ANTIBES.   Its beach and shining harbor with boats reflected in the calm blue water form a perfect picture with the old Fort Carre of Antibes on a small peninsula in the background.

A few miles further along near the coast is a small village, BIOT, where glassware has been made for only fifteen years and already has quite a reputation.   A visit to a glass factory is a must and the types of glassware to see and purchase are amazing.   They vary from the usual types to the Provincial "caleres" or "ponons-bottles" that have two long necks and are only used for drinking "a la regalade."

Driving further you will discover yourself at CAGNES SUR MER only a few miles south of Saint Paul de Vence; this is a port town struggling to resemble the other coastal cities.   HAUT DE CAGNES, an old section located on the hill, has charm and character.   The Chateau Grimaldi was built by

Raynier Grimaldi in 1309, sovereign of Monaco and a French Admiral. Also of interest is the Musee Renoir, where Renoir spent his last days. LE CAGNARD, a hotel-restaurant, is tucked away in the old village and its terrace dining is both atmospheric and excellent in its quality and presentation.

Continuing for only four miles you arrive again at Nice, a city where you can always discover something exciting, perhaps something that you missed before. Travel round the peninsula of Nice on the low road and discover the picturesque ancient port of Nice tucked around its own sheltered port. The old town contrasts with the new and will add to your memories and photos.

Leaving Nice in the direction of Menton, you not only have a choice between the "high" road and the "low" road, but also of the "middle" road, or you can do as I did and switch off and on among the three. The roads all run somewhat parallel to each other following the contours of the coast. The Grand Corniche or "high" road was built by Napoleon and passes through two picturesque towns, ROQUEBRUNE and LA TUURBIE. The Moyenne Corniche or "middle" road is a lovely modern road. The Corniche Inferieure or "low" road was built in the Eighteenth Century by the prince of Monaco and enables you to visit ST. JEAN CAP FERRAT, the wealthy community of BEAULIEU and the small state of MONACO. Take the "Low" road out of Nice and you will discover what many have already claimed for their luxurious hideaways ... the peninsula of St Jean Cap Fettat. Drive through this residential district and scout out the villas and celebrities, and then round down to the coastal village of BEAULIEU SUR MER. To fully appreciate the luxury and grandeur of the Riviera let yourself be pampered at LA RESERVE. Set right on the Mediterranean with a magnificent terrace restaurant, it is perhaps one of the Riviera's highlights. The restaurant of La Reserve was founded by the Lottier family in 1894 on the same spot that it occupies today and it is perhaps the most elegant "restaurant with rooms" that I have encountered in France! Its reputation as one of the country's most accredited restaurants is now almost a tradition and acknowledged by celebrities and royalty from its earliest beginnings. You will be expertly catered to both in the dining room and hotel. The restaurant with floor to ceiling windows overlooking the salt-water pool and ocean, is bordered by an outside terrace where lunch and dinner are served in the balmy summer months.   The pool is heated in the winter and is surrounded by a private dock where yachts are moored while guests dine.   La Reserve's clients not only return year after year but also request the same room.   There are fifty bedrooms in all, each traditionally furnished plus three apartments which have a sitting room and private balcony.

As the road leaves Beaulieau Sur Mer in the direction of MONACO it hugs the mountain and cuts under and around the hazards and rock.   MENTON is a bustling but charming port town on the Italian border.   Return in the direction of Nice via the "middle" road.   It affords magnificent views and it winds past the medieval village of ROQUEBRUNE and on to the village of EZE.   Of all the perched towns, Eze will remain my favorite.   It is a quaint medieval village with cobble-stoned streets, overlooking the sea.   (Park your car where you can below the village and leave your luggage to be collected by porters.)   At its peak you will discover the fabulous CHATEAU DE LA CHEVRE D'OR, where you may happily settle down for the night.

For more than a thousand years this chateau has soaked up the sun and looked down upon the beautiful blue water associated with the Cote d'Azur. With restorations, the additions of antiques and touches to decorate the walls, the chateau came alive once again as the magnificent Hotel de la Chevre d'Or. The attractive rooms, attentive service, superb cuisine, views and pool with surrounding patios wedged into the hillside make the chateau a hotel which will be hard to leave but delightful to return to.

Stationed at Eze and the Chateau de la Chevre d'Or, you can choose your own time to explore the three corniches and all the port towns. Take advantage of the beautiful beaches and warm blue waters, gamble at the casino in Monaco, enjoy the night life of the cities, investigate the various restaurants-just be sure to let me know what you find and have a wonderful time.

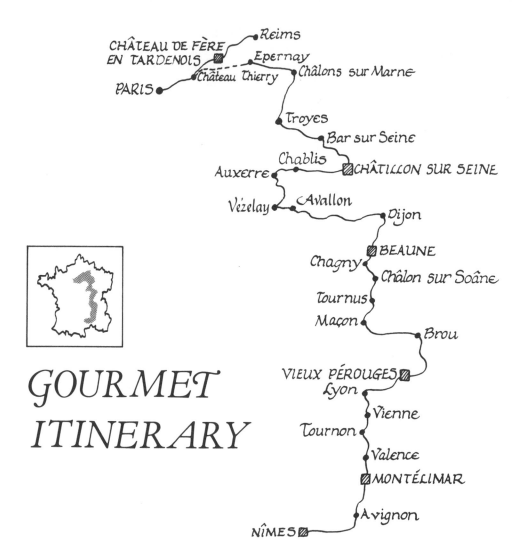

Reims

CHÂTEAU DE FÈRE
EN TARDENOIS

PARIS

Château Thierry

Epernay

Châlons sur Marne

Troyes

Bar sur Seine

Chablis

Auxerre

CHÂTILLON SUR SEINE

Vézelay

Avallon

Dijon

BEAUNE

Chagny

Châlon sur Soâne

Tournus

Mâcon

Brou

VIEUX PÉROUGES

Lyon

Vienne

Tournon

Valence

MONTÉLIMAR

Avignon

NÎMES

GOURMET ITINERARY

WINE AND DINE YOUR WAY THROUGH the "gastronomique" areas of France. Travel through the regions of Champagne and Burgundy and down the Rhone River Valley. The wines are plentiful and delicious; the cuisine of Burgundy is considered to be the best in all of France. Enjoy the luxury of visiting the wine cellars and selecting your own vintage.

I will suggest some specific wine cellars to visit wherever possible. However, most of the chateaux are private residences, and although you might not find their name listed on a tourist pamphlet, if a sign "degustation" is posted, you will always be more than welcome. The families are dependent on selling wine and they are delighted to have you sample theirs. Experience their style of life, if only for an afternoon: join them in the fields, pick some ripe grapes and be amazed at the home method of producing wine.

DAY I   FERE EN TARDENOIS   Chateau de Fere en Tardenois

Leave Paris for the Champagne district. On the way is the town of CHATEAU THIERRY, site of American and British memorials of the First World War.

The Champagne region, whose soil and climate are important factors in making champagne the wine it is, is only ninety miles northeast of Paris. It centers around a small range of hills rising from a plain of chalk and divided by the winding Marne River. Unlike Burgundy, Champagne and the quality of it are not derived solely from the area but also from the manufacturing process. It is the dose of sugar or "bead" that makes the bubbles, and the smaller the bead, the better the champagne. The quantity of sugar is sometimes increased to cover the poorer qualities of the wine. The essence of champagne is the blending of several different grades; a branded wine, it is known by the maker and not by the vineyard. There are three distinct zones for the 55,000 acres in Champagne: the "Montagne de Reims", the "Vallee de la Marne" and "Cote des Blancs." Each produces a characteristic essential to the classic champagne blend.

The old cathedral town of REIMS was named the capital of France's champagne region. Although it is out of the vineyard district, its underground chalk tunnels serve as a storage place for the many bottles of sparkling wine. Take advantage of the many renowned champagne cellars by visiting and sampling their creations. For more details go to the tourist office near the train station; they will be able to supply you with information as to which winery will allow you to visit on that day. There are a number of cellars in the Champ de Mars quarter and at the end of Saint Nicaise-chalk cellars, in particular. Also before leaving Reims be sure to see the famous cathedral Notre Dame, an exceptional Thirteenth Century monument where most of the French kings were crowned.

Champagne is associated with celebrations and celebrate is exactly what you should do upon arrival at the lovely hotel CHATEAU DE FERE EN TARDENOIS. Tucked away beside the ruins of a castle, the location is peaceful and the views are splendid. The restaurant has an excellent menu with delicacies such as "turbot au champagne" and "ecrivisses fine champagne", and the pastries and fruit tarts are too tempting to resist. There are twenty individually decorated and appealing bedrooms with beautiful fabrics covering the walls. The beds are large and comfortable and even the bathrooms are spacious. It is hard to narrow my selection of favorite rooms down to a few, but if I must, I will choose rooms #29, 30 and 12. The latter two are large, lovely apartments, and #29 is in the tower, dating back to 1527. There are windows on two sides wedged between thick walls and overlooking the valley. The white lace bedspread and pink and cream wall paper make the room feminine and dainty.

DAY II   CHATILLON SUR SEINE   Hotel de la Cote D'Or

This morning drive to the center of the old province of Champagne, Epernay, which is in the second of the distinct Chanpagne zones and seventeen miles south of Reims. On the southern banks of the Marne, it is a small town surrounded by vineyards, the best of which are located above the dear town of Ay. In addition to visiting the cellars of Epernay (Moet et Chandon, 18, avenue de Champagne; Mercier, 75 avenue de Champagne; de Castellane, 57, rue de Verdun), see the interesting museum on wine in the ancient Perrier chateau. From Epernay drive southeast towards Chalons sur Marne, through the third zone of Cote des Blancs.

Continue south through the major city of Troyes and another major champagne town, Bar sur Seine, and on to Chatillon sur Seine. The drive for today ends at the HOTEL DE LA COTE D'OR. M. and Mme. Richards, a friendly, handsome, young couple own and run this wonderful hotel. Mme Richards has tastefully decorated all twelve rooms, adding bright touches with each new year. Approximately half of the rooms are with bath. Freshen up and then the restaurant's tempting menu will make you realize just how hungry you are. Charming as the restaurant may be, tomorrow morning enjoy your breakfast in the garden; fresh air, aromatic coffee, hot rolls coated with homemade butter and jam are an ideal way to begin your day.

DAY III   BEAUNE   Hotel le Cep

This morning marks the end of the Champagne region and the beginning of the Burgundy. Within the area titled "Burgundy" there are a number of distinct wines; the region produces a variety of whites, reds, and roses.   Burgundy wines vary; the soil, the grape, the climate, and the individual vineyards which make them are all responsible for the distinctions.   "Burgundy" is a misused term and there are too many imitations unjustly claiming the title; it can only come from France where conditions are unique.   The "real" Burgundy wine is not plentiful but it is truly great!

From Chatillon sur Seine it is a lovely drive to CHABLIS, and directly across the Seine River are seven small vineyards.   In this happy, serene, country town you can taste the wine from an appropriate "tastevin"-this is a small, shallow silver dish that exposes the qualities and characteristics of the wine.   Dauvissat and Servin are particularly good wines to sample at the Caveau Chablisien.

Continue on to AUXERRE and then head south to AVALLON and the famous HOTEL DE LA POSTE.   I hope you are hungry, for this ancient postal stop now serves some of the finest cuisine in France.   Here you can order lunch and have your first taste of what the Burgundy kitchens offer.   Every dish here is considered a speciality but best of all are "timbale d'homard gourmande", "pintadeau roti", and "flambe a la riche."

VEZELAY is just a few miles from Avallon and well worth a visit.   A walled, medieval, hilltop village it has a some interesting shops and galleries to visit.   Encircling the ramparts is an abandoned road that now makes for a wonderful footpath and affords a delightful walk with valley views opening up in all directions.

Leave the isolated region of Chablis and drive towards the heart of Burgundy, known as the Cote d'Or which beings at Dijon and ends at Chagny and is responsible for Burgundy's finest wines.   Today this "Golden slope" is divided into two divisions.   Three-quarters of the great red wines are produced in the northern Cote de Nuits; the remainder of the reds and the great white wines are from the southern Cote de Beaune.   From Chagny almost to Lyon is an area more generally known for the wines of Southern Burgundy which are divided into three cotes: Cote de Chalonnais, Cote de Maconnais and Cote de Beaujolais.

From Avallon head for Dijon on the trip of the Cote de Nuits.   Dijon is known for its wine as well as for its mustard. Ancient capital of the Dukes of Burgundy, it has a palace to wander through and traces of history to experience.

South of Dijon is the colorful old city of BEAUNE. It is the capital of Burgundy, and many would say of the world. Beaune was also the residence of the Dukes of Burgundy; installed in their Fifteenth Century house is a marvelous museum on the history and cultivation of Burgundy wines.

HOTEL LE CEP is a wood-framed building blending easily with the character of the walled town. It is a small hotel but can play a large part in establishing wonderful memories for your trip in and around Beaune. The rooms are all decorated with well-chosen antiques. There are old beamed ceilings throughout the hotel and even the winding staircase creaks every so often to add to its authentic yet relaxed atmosphere. Simple meals will be prepared on request and served in the vaulted cellar where one large table constitutes the restaurant.

DAY IV   PEROUGES   Ostellerie du Vieux Perouges

POMMARD, MEURSAULT and PULIGNY-MONTRACHET are important wine towns which lie between Beaune and Chagny. Chagny has a marvelous hotel-restaurant, the LAMELOISE. If you have stopped at every wine cellar en route it might be best that you do take a break, and it is probably nearing lunch time anyway. The restaurant Lameloise is a fine choice.

The drive, now bordered by the Maconnais vineyards, continues south through the town of CHALON and weaves along the Saone River. The route passes through Tournus with its church of Saint Philibert and on to the Seventeenth Century town of Macon. If it is possible, take your mind off wines now and begin concentrating on tonight's destination, PEROUGES. At Macon leave the Saone and drive east. At the town of Brou, with its great monastery and church, begin the drive south. VIEUX PEROUGES, a medieval village, has cobble-stoned streets (explore the character of the village on Place du Tilleul and along rue des Rondes), art and pottery workshops and boutiques.

OSTELLERIE DU VIEUX PEROUGES and its excellent restaurant are located in one of Perouges' many old, wood-timbered homes that no longer stand erect, but rather lean out over the narrow streets. The hotel has twenty-five rooms in two separate buildings; fifteen are furnished with antiques, and the others are more simple, yet still inviting.

DAY V   MONTELIMAR   Relais de L'Empereur

This morning the road leads to the metropolitan city of LYON and back to the wine valley.   Lyon is the home of the silk industry and has a museum on the history of fabrics, among others.   Its restaurants are the best in the world, and depending on your mood, you might want to visit the old Gallo-Roman quarter and have lunch here, or you might prefer to simply continue south back to the quiet country along the Rhone River.   Geographically, Lyon is where the Rhone wine region begins.

Along the course of the Rhone River the countryside changes from oak forest to the herbal scrub and olive groves so characteristic of Provence. Following suit, the vineyards of the Rhone fall into two groups: northern and southern. In the north, the Cote de Rotie and Condrieu are the two principal vineyards, and in the south the wine generally falls under the title of the Cote du Rhone. The first great wine vineyards lie thirty miles south of Lyon across the river from the old Roman town of VIENNE. The Crozes-Hermitage, the Hermitage, the Tain, the Cornas and Saint Peray vineyards are passed before arriving at VALANCE. It is built on terraces overlooking the Rhone, has a number of Roman monuments, and is the location of the famous restaurant PIC, where you might want to have lunch if you did not stop at Lyon.

Gourmet Itinerary

For the fifth night on the "wine and dine" tour, Montelimar and the RELAIS DE L'EMPEREUR serve as an ideal place to stop. The "empereur" of this fantastic relais is Napoleon who stayed in room #15 on four different occasions with four different "amours." Throughout the hotel there are paintings, stained-glass windows and artifacts all relating to his life. M Roger Latry, the owner, has a wonderful sense of humor and that marvelous gift of being able to make his guests comfortable and relaxed. He will be proud to show you every item concerning Napoleon. His beautiful daughter tends the reception desk, and he and his wife are often in the lounge-bar conversing with guests. The bartender has four special "Napoleon" drinks, at least one of which you should try, if not all. The restaurant is excellent; I was distracted by a number of tasty dishes-large steaks, "agneau de tricastin", "filets de sole Francis Latry".

DAY VI   NIMES   Hotel Imperator

Leaving Montelimar the road soon approaches PROVENCE. The last day and stretch of your trip will pass through the major vineyards of Rasteau, Taval, Chateauneuf du Pape, through AVIGNON and on to NIMES. It seems only appropriate that in a region of France's finest wines is also the location of a superior chateau-hotel with an outstanding restaurant, the HOSTELLERIE FINES ROCHES which would prove an ideal luncheon selection. If the weather is nice you might want to consider packing a picnic and enjoying lunch and the view from the ruins of the Chateauneuf du Pape castle.

AVIGNON, the temporary seat of the Papacy in exile, is one of Europe's most beautiful and interesting medieval cities. The Fourteenth Century Palace of the Popes is striking, grand and dominates the walled city.

Only a short distance from Avignon is the lively and gay city of NIMES. The HOTEL IMPERATOR across the park is a very fine hotel which has managed to isolate some peace and quiet in the middle of a large city.   All the rooms are with bath or shower.   Each is spacious and artistically decorated with antiques. The rooms facing the garden are only 11 francs more and well worth it; some have balconies at no extra cost, so you should make a point of asking for one.

Now, a few pounds heavier and imbued with grander knowledge of wine (or perhaps just with wine imbibed), your "wine and dine" tour comes to an end. Your own travel arrangements can easily be made of out Nimes.

Marlenheim

10 KM

Molsheim

5 KM

Rosheim

8 KM

Obernai

12 KM

Barr

3 KM

Andlau

14 KM D35

Chartenois

13 KM

Strasbourg

N 83 38 KM

Sélestat

Ribeauvillé

4.5 KM

Riquewihr

5 KM

Kayersberg

N 415 10 KM

N 83 17 KM

N 415

Colmar

Turckheim

19 KM

ALSACE

Munster Valley

Hohneck

Pt. Ballon

ROUTES DES CRETES

ROUFFACH

N 83 12 KM

Quebwiller

Vieil Armand

Cernay

Mulhouse

THE ALSACIAN REGION BORDERS GERMANY and as a result the language has a definite German accent. The people tend to be physically broad and tall. The homes resemble those of the Tyrol. Rooftops ornamented with storks dot the horizon. The wine is German but made in the French manner. Beginning in March, tens of thousands of storks break their journey for the African continent in Alsace. Then or any time Alsace has character, the region is dramatically beautiful and a visit is rewarding.

DAY I: ROUFFACH   Chateau D'Isenbourg

Depart from MULHOUSE, a fairly large industrial city. The first few hours in Alsace will be spent following the Route des Cretes, which winds along the Vosges and through its valleys. Strategically located, this road was constructed by the French during the First World War to ensure communications between the different valleys.

Thirty thousand German and French soldiers died on the ledges of Vieil Armand during that war. A beautiful landmark, it has splendid views but unfortunately many sad memories.

Grand Ballon, the Vosges' highest peak, deserves a hike. From its summit the Vosges range, the Black Forest, and, on a clear day, the Jura and the Alps can be seen.

Hohneck is perhaps one of the most celebrated summits of the Vosges. Again, the panorama is splendid. From Hohneck this itinerary veers toward the wine road. En route you will pass through the Munster Valley, where the farmland is fenced by the mountains themselves.

Reaching the wine road, N83, drive south to CHATEAU D'ISENBOURG in ROUFFACH, the one outstanding hotel I discovered in the Alsacian region. It is an ideal spot to unpack and settle while you make trips to the various small Alsacian towns, visiting the cellars and sampling the wine during the day.

During the Middle Ages the Chateau d'Isenbourg was the cherished home of the "prince bishops" of Strasbourg and more recently it was owned by wealthy wine growers. On the hillside above the town of Rouffach, the chateau is still surrounded by its own vineyards. You can appropriately savor your delicious meal and fine Alsacian wines in the vaulted wine cellars which now serve as a very pleasant restaurant. There are thirty-three rooms, nine of which are new. A number of rooms are exceptionally elegant with impressive, handpainted ceilings. Room #1, a beautiful apartment, and #2, which is not an apartment but quite spacious, are two such rooms. Room #14 is not priced as an apartment but is practically the same size and also is quite lovely. The chateau has a large pool as well.

The Route de Vin is at the base of the mountains which are dressed with vineyards. In the stretch between Rouffach and Obernai, you will find wine is King, dominating and affecting the character and personality of each town and the life style of the people. In the northern section from Obernai to Marlenheim neither tradition nor culture has suffered in the least; costumes are predominant, and festivals and holidays are still adhered to. At intervals buildings group together forming towns, each town a charming stroll. Of them, OBERNAI is said to be the prettiest, then RIBEAUVILLE, RIQUEWIHR, KAYERSBERG, TURKHEIM and EQUISHEIM not far behind. COLMAR is a larger but attractive town on the River Luach. The Unterlinden Museum and the old part of town with its streets bordered by "true" Alascian homes give the key to the region.

STRASBOURG, directly on the border, is a beautiful city and possibly the most convenient point to end your trip. The walls of Strasbourg's gothic cathedral absorbed much of the city's history. A walk through the old city will take you back to another era. The Rue du Bain aux Plantes is bordered by many 16th and 17th century homes of the Alsacian Renaissance; this quarter is where the craftsmen gathered and left their mark, in the best preserved section of Strasbourg, referred to as "La Petite France". Transportation facilities are numerous and, until the moment you depart, the trip will remain exciting.

Take your time visiting the region, enjoying the wines, style and color of the life and culture. If possible, plan your visit during the wine harvest, as then there will be that much more to see and experience and remember.

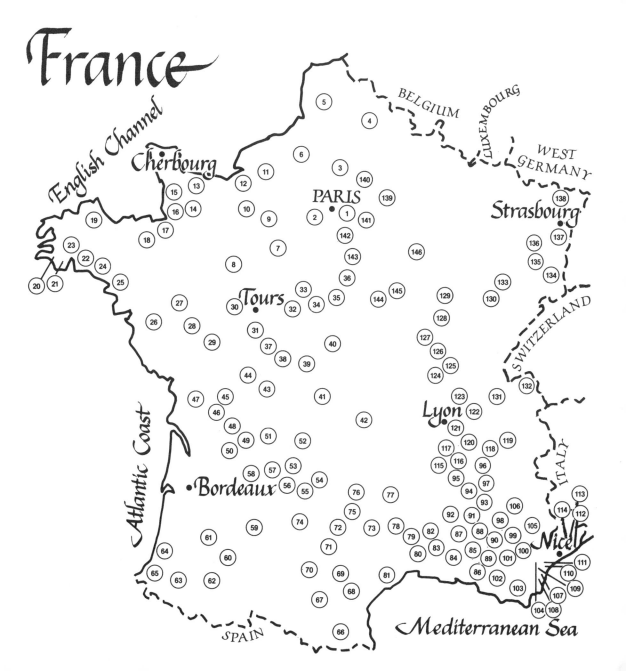

INDEX OF HOTELS REFERENCED by MAP NUMBER

INDEX OF HOTELS REFERENCED by MAP NUMBER   117

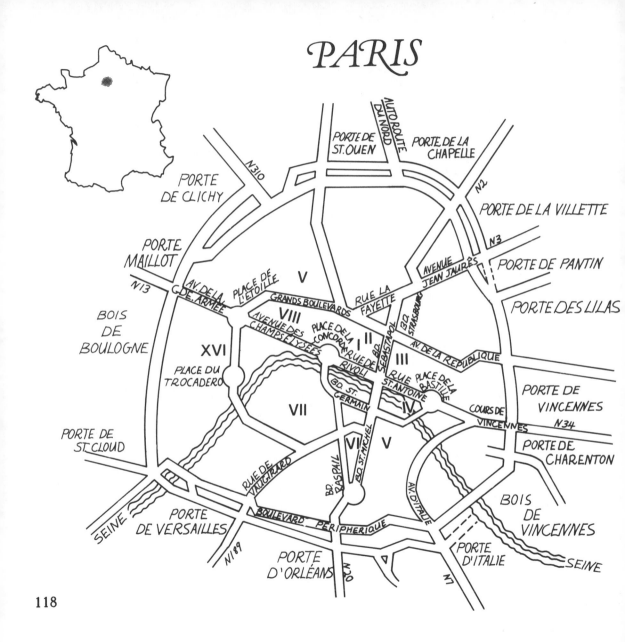

PARIS, BEAUTIFUL AND SOPHISTICATED, lives up to her reputation. Sectioned off by arrondissements, there is not one interesting area to visit, but, rather many. Each arrondissement has its own character, flavor and style. It is almost as if "Paris" were a name given to a group of clustering cities. Depending on the reason for your trip or the number of times you've been to Paris, each arrondissement will have its own appeal and attraction.

I am including descriptions of selected arrondissements and a few small hotels found within each. I have chosen the arrondissements I feel hold the most interest for the tourist and recommend some charming, almost "country" hotels in the city of Paris. Following the hotel descriptions are some restaurant suggestions. With each visit to Paris undoubtedly the most enjoyable "attraction" to research are the restaurants. It is never a question of whether one will discover any, but in a city noted worldwide for its cuisine, it is simply a question of how many ... governed by the number of nights one has to "research". I include in this edition a few of my favorites, ones that I always gravitate to, and for me some exciting new discoveries. On a recent trip, with the delightful company of a close friend, our evenings were dedicated to the research of the palate!

FIRST ARRONDISSEMENT

The FIRST ARRONDISSEMENT is an ideal location for "first-timers" in Paris. As the heart of the city, many of the major tourist attractions are situated here: Place de la Concorde, Rue de Rivoli, the Madeleine, elegant and expensive shops along the well-known Rue du Faubourg Saint Honore, the Tuileries and the Louvre. Find a hotel here and you will never have to deal with the Metro or the stubborn taxi-cab drivers. You can take romantic walks along the Seine or in the Tuileries Gardens. Excitement was born on the Champs Elysees, a wide boulevard that stretches from the Place de la Concorde to the Arc de Triomphe.

In the First Arrondissement it is possible to see and experience so many of the different aspects of the city that if you have not spent time in Paris before, this is the ONLY place to begin.

HOTELS IN THE FIRST ARRONDISSEMENT

HOTEL VENDOME: The Hotel Vendome is a small distinguished hotel. Located on the same Place as the famous Ritz Hotel, designer shops and prestigious financial offices, the Vendome is a favorite of many.   The varying sizes of the bedrooms are reflected in their price, but, all are attractive and comfortable.   On the second floor are a bar and simple restaurant; modern in their decor.   The entry of the hotel is small but is the base for the delightful receptionist and very accommodating concierge.   Service at the Vendome is very professional, yet personal.

Hotelier: M. Andre, 1, Place Vendome; 75001 Paris; Tel: 260.32.84,
Telex: 680403, 35 Rooms, Expensive, Credit Cards: AX

HOTEL MAYFAIR: On a small street just off the Rue de Rivoli is a lovely hotel combining modern comforts with elegance.   The rooms are pleasing in their decor and service is attentive.   The hotel does not have a restaurant, which might prove to be more fortunate than not, for just a block away are a number of cozy family restaurants with delicious, plentiful and reasonably priced meals. (Le Soufflet; L'Escure; Restaurant Faure; all on the Rue Mont Thabor.)

3, Rue Rouget sur l'Isle, 75001 Paris, Tel: 260.38.14, Telex: 240037
53 Rooms, Expensive, Credit Cards: All Major

HOTEL DES TUILERIES: Small attractive rooms and a courteous welcome await you at the Hotel des Tuileries under the direction of Mme Vidal.   The hotel is separated from the Rue de Rivoli and the Louvre by the wonderful shopping street St. Honore.   A delightful breakfast is the only meal served.

M. Poulle-Vidal, 10 Rue St Hyacinthe, 75001 Paris, Tel: 261.04.17
Telex: 240744, 28 Rooms, Moderate, Credit Cards: VS

RESTAURANTS IN THE FIRST ARRONDISSEMENT

LE SOUFFLE: If you are fond of soufflets this is most definitely the place to come. The restaurant has a fantastic selection and is reasonable and cute.

36, Rue Mont Thabor, 75001 Paris, Tel: 260.27.19,
Closed Sundays, Credit Cards: All Major

L'ESCURE: L'Escure is truly a bargain and the food is very good and portions are plentiful. (Try the bouef bourguigonne and the rasberries smothered in fresh, thick cream). L'Escure is particularly fun because of the friendly atmosphere set by the waiters who manage to maneuver under the garlic strands amongst and around the many tables squeezed into this little hideaway.

7, Rue de Mondavi, 75001 Paris, Tel: 742.36.69, Closed in August

ANDRE FAURE: This restaurant has a family style atmosphere, serves large quantities, (they leave everything on the table and you take your own portions), the food is delicious, and seems to be a "hang out" for businessmen at lunch time.

40, Rue Mont Thabor, 75001 Paris, Tel: 073.39.15

WILLIAMS AND SMITH: (Yes the book store!) Above Williams and Smith there is a darling restaurant, where you can order tea and delicious scones. It is a great stopping place when your feet tire.

Rue de Rivoli (near the Place de la Concorde), 75001 Paris

LE GRAND VEFOUR: A very beautiful, romantic restaurant that has been popular for centuries. As a 1760's cafe it appealed to Napoleon and later became a favorite of a number of artists and writers.

17 rue Beaujolais, 75001 Paris, Tel: 296.56.27,
Closed Aug, Sat & Sun, Credit Cards: AX

ANGELINA'S: For truly the most sinfully delicious hot chocolate anywhere! Lovely pastries to sample in the morning and sandwiches and salads for lunch or tea time.

On the Rue de Rivoli, 75001 Paris

FOURTH ARRONDISSEMENT

The highlight of the FOURTH ARRONDISSEMENT is the Ile de Saint Louis. It is a charming island neighboring the Ile de la Cite. There are many enticing antique and craft shops. Crossing the bridge in either direction, it is a short walk along the quai to the Latin Quarter or a pleasant stroll to the Louvre. The hotels are quaint and inviting and at night, at least, the streets are quiet.

HOTELS IN THE FOURTH ARRONDISSEMENT

HOTEL DE LUTECE: The charm of the Ile de Saint Louis has penetrated the walls of the Hotel de Lutece. It is obvious from the moment you are welcomed into the foyer with its burning fire, flowers and antiques. The rooms are all comfortable and inviting. Room #53 is a duplex and the largest of all.

Hotelier: M. Buffat, 65, Rue Saint Louis en L'Ile, 75004 Paris, Tel: 326.23.52, 23 Rooms, Moderate, No Credit Cards

HOTEL SAINT LOUIS: This is a small hotel with atmosphere located on the Ile de Saint Louis, near antique and pastry shops. The rooms are not large, but they are simple and nicely furnished. #51 and #52 are doubles with bath and #53 is a double with shower. Madame Record describes her hotel as "if in another era ... 50 years behind ... no T.V., no telephone, no elevator!". Guests leave only praises in the register with vows to return. The presense of the Records is a welcomed advantage as they are efficient and very caring of their guests.

Their hospitality far exceeds any other on the island.

Andree et Guy Record, 75, Rue Saint Louis en Ile, 75004 Paris
Tel: 634.04.08, 25 Rooms, Moderate, No Credit Cards

HOTEL DEUX ILES: Captured in a 17th century house is the quaint and charming Hotel Deux Iles. Interior decorator, Roland Buffat, responsible for the already popular Hotel Lutece, has employed cheerful prints, bamboo and reed in the furnishings; included an open fire-place to serve as a focal point for a cozy retreat or rendez-vous and expanded a central area into a garden of plants and flowers. The result, an unusual and harmonious blend of color, furnishings and an inviting atmosphere. Paris has once again profited from the talents of Roland Buffat.

Hotelier: M. Buffat, 59 Rue Saint Louis En L'Ile, 75004 Paris,
Tel: 326.13.35, 17 Rooms, Moderate, No Credit Cards

RESTAURANTS IN THE FOURTH ARRONDISSEMENT

BRASSERIE DE L'ILE SAINT LOUIS: A popular spot, crowded with island locals happy for an order of sauerkraut, sausages, munster cheese and a refreshing beer. Reasonable and friendly atmosphere.

55 Quai de Bourbon, 75004 Paris, Tel: 354.02.59, No Credit Cards

FIFTH, SIXTH AND SEVENTH ARRONDISSEMENTS

All three, the FIFTH, SIXTH AND SEVENTH, are the ARRONDISSEMENTS which comprise the ever-popular Latin Quarter. Here you will find activity and companionship abound. There are creperies and other shops, the Sorbonne and its students, antique shops and art galleries, and so many restaurants, all promising "favorites" to be discovered. At night many of the small streets are blocked off and the real life of the area begins.

The left bank of the Latin Quarter is separated from the right bank by the Seine and the Isle de la Cite. The grandeur of Notre Dame is overpowering when illuminated at night. Do not overlook the St. Chapelle and its praised stained-glass windows. Along the quai are many secondhand book stalls. In the Latin Quarter there is a constant wave of activity. It is a bustling area but there are several hotels where you can find a room and close out the noise.

HOTELS IN THE FIFTH ARRONDISSEMENT

HOTEL COLBERT: Rue de l'Hotel Colbert and the hotel are a find in that they are small and quiet, yet near Notre Dame and in the center of the activity of the Latin Quarter. The forty hotel rooms are small and cozy but diverse. Room # 12 is a gold room with a double bed and bath. # 19 is green with twin beds and bath, and # 11 is a red, rustic room with a double bed and bath. All three are particularly nice rooms.

Hotelier: M. J. Canteloup, 7, Rue de l'Hotel Colbert, 75005 Paris, Tel: 325.85.65, Telex: 260690, 40 rooms, Moderate, Credit Cards: AX, VS

RESTAURANTS IN THE FIFTH ARRONDISSEMENT

DODIN-BOUFFANT: An unpretentious and excellent fish restaurant. This a favorite of a very particular few and has earned their repeated praise! Highly recommended as an appetizer: Salade Folle.

25 rue Frederic-Sauton, 75005 Paris, Tel: 325.25.14, Credit Cards: VS

TOUR D'ARGENT: World famous for excellent cuisine and a sophisticated atmosphere, the Tour D'Argent is also very expensive.

15, Quai Tournelle, 75005 Paris, Tel: 354.23.31, Credit Cards: AX,DC

COUPE-CHOU: Very romantic, cozy decor. Heavy with beams, intimate corners are lit with candles. The food was good, however the service disappointing.

11 rue Lanneau, 75005 Paris, Tel: 633.68.69, Credit Cards: AX

HOTELS IN THE SIXTH ARRONDISSEMENT

HOTEL SCANDINAVIA: My favorite, Hotel Scandinavia has knights in armor in the corners, beamed ceilings and antique furnishings. A number of the rooms have majestic, four poster beds. It is a special hideaway with qualities and characteristics often hard to find in big cities ... a real "gem."

27, Rue de Tournon, 75006 Paris, Tel: 329.67.20, 22 Rooms
Moderate, Closed Aug, No Credit Cards

L'HOTEL: L'Hotel is a colorful and glamorous hotel whose expensive lodgings attract many celebrities. Its presence, on a small side street in the heart of the Latin Quarter, is barely noticeable. A small door and name plaque are the only clues. Inside the hotel is graced by a beautiful open rotunda, and scattered about are fountains, plants and birds. Although expensive, this hotel's ornately decorated rooms draw many appreciative guests. There are two spectacular suites with kitchenettes that occupy the top two floors and look out across the rooftops of Paris. The Oscar Wilde chamber boasts its own terrace and is always reserved well in advance. For dining the restaurant is popular with a sophisticated late night crowd. The piano bar opens at 6:00pm and in the restaurant the last order is accepted at 1:00am.

Director: J.F. Grand, 13 Rue des Beaux Arts, 75006 Paris, Telex: 270870
Tel: 325.27.22, 27 Rooms, Very Expensive

HOTEL D'ANGLETERRE: The former British Embassy has belonged to the Berthier Family since 1910. They have added all the modern conveniences: baths, WC in each room, elevator, etc., and converted it into a lovely hotel. While the location is in the center of the Latin Quarter, the rooms, overlooking an inner, quiet courtyard are peaceful and calm.

44, Rue Jacob, 75006 Paris, Tel:260.34.72,
33 Rooms, Moderate, No Credit Cards

HOTEL ABBAYE ST-GERMAIN: Suggested by readers on numerous occasions, the Hotel Abbaye St-Germain is definitely a hotel deserving of recommendation. Mme Lafortune has achieved a delightful countryside ambiance utilizing her tasteful decorating choices to accent the charm and character of this restored 18th century residence. Serviced by an elevator, the bedrooms, if not large, are pleasantly appointed and each is equipped with private bath. Breakfast or refreshments can be enjoyed in the serene setting of a central patio-garden.

Hotelier: M et Mme Lafortune, 10, Rue Cassette, 75006 Paris, Tel: 544.38.11, 45 Rooms, Moderate, No Credit Cards

RESTAURANTS IN THE SIXTH ARRONDISSEMENT

DOMINIQUE: Dominique is a marvelous Russian Restaurant, a fact which is confirmed by the number of Russians who gather here. It is a fun restaurant with atmosphere.

19, Rue Brea, 75006, Tel: 327.08.80, Closed July, All Credit Cards

BRASSERIE LIPP: A brasserie is ideal if you would simply prefer a light lunch or snack and Lipp is one of the more famous in Paris.

151 Blvd Saint Germain, 75006 Paris, Tel: 548.53.91

LE BELIER: L'Hotel's restaurant attracts a very sophisticated late night crowd. Piano bar opens at 6pm and the last restaurant order is taken at 1am.

13 Rue des Beaux Arts, 75006 Paris, Tel: 325.27.22

HOTELS IN THE SEVENTH ARRONDISSEMENT

HOTEL SAINT SIMON: Hotel Saint Simon is a quaint hotel where all the personnel speak English due to the many British and American guests. The bedrooms are cheerful and sweet in their decor. Some have private balconies and others overlook the small courtyard and garden in the back. I was informed that the largest and best double rooms are 24, 25, and 14 and that 42, a twin bedded room has its own terrace. The hallways of the Saint Simon are spotlessly clean; hung with nice prints and the delightful entry is welcoming and brightened by geraniums. I was pleased to discover that both day and night, you are away from the noises of the city.

Hotelier: M. Lalisse, 14 Rue Saint Simon, 75007 Paris,
Tel: 548.35.66, 34 Rooms, Moderate, No Credit Cards

HOTEL DE L'UNIVERSITE: Enchanting, the Hotel De L'Universite is characteristically deserving of the Left Bank location and reknown. This renovated three hundred year-old residence sadly affords visitors to Paris only twenty-eight bedrooms. Its size, however, does contribute to the atmosphere of a Parisien hideaway as does the delightful courtyard, glassed in garden and many antiques. Tapestries, beams and wooden doors warm the entry and the touches of brass are brillantly polished. Although not serviced by the elevator, the three top floor rooms are the most deluxe and room number 54 profits from a private terrace.

22 Rue Universite, 75007 Paris, Tel: 261.09.39, Telex: 260717
27 Rooms, Moderate, No Credit Cards

RESTAURANTS IN THE SEVENTH ARRONDISSEMENT

JULEN ET LE PETIT: Small restaurant, very French in its decor. Art gallery posters cover the street front windows and crisp white linens dress the tables indoors. Take notice of the chest of drawers in the corner where locals store personal napkins.

40 Rue de l'Universite, 75007 Paris, Closed August

L'ARCHESTRATE: Exceptional service and a superb menu make L'Archestrate an elegant and memorable dining experience. Reservations are difficult to obtain, but we were lucky and arrived early. There is no bar but we were happy to wait in the reception area. The Maitre D' apologized to us and offered complimentary drinks and a sampling of delicate hor d'ouevres! Exceptional!

84 rue Varenne, tel: 551.47.33,
Closed 28 Jul- 21 Aug, Credit Cards: AX, VS

EIGHTH ARRONDISSEMENT

Crowned by the Arc de Triomphe and boasting the Champs Elysees, the EIGHTH ARRONDISSEMENT is a bustle of activity twenty-four hours of the day. There are shops, sidewalk cafes, nightclubs, movies, and endless people watching.

HOTELS IN THE EIGHTH ARRONDISSEMENT

HOTEL LANCASTER: Hotel Lancaster is one of the truly elegant and luxurious hotels of Paris. Prices are high but reflect the magnificence of the rooms, so lovely in fact that you may never want to venture outside. The restaurant is intimate and the service discreet and personal.

Hotelier: J. Sinclair, 7 Rue Berri, 75008 Paris, Tel: 359.90.43,
Telex: 640891, 58 Rooms, Very Expensive, Credit Cards: All Major

HOTEL SAN REGIS: Small, traditional and intimate, the San Regis was once a fashionable town house. It is now perhaps the best value for a first class hotel in Paris. With exclusive boutiques and embassies as its sophisticated neighbors, the hotel maintains an air of simple yet authentic elegance. From the exterior it is easy to pass this marvelous hotel by. A small sign is the only thing that advertises its presense. Beyond the small entry is a comfortable lounge area and small dining room. Here one can enjoy a quiet drink and/or an often welcome light meal (soups, salads, sandwiches). The bedrooms are large, handsomely furnished and the bathrooms are very modern and thoughtfully stocked. Huge double doors buffer sounds from other rooms. The rooms that front the Rue Jean Goujon favor a view across to the tip of the towering Eifel Tower, but rooms on the courtyard are sheltered from any street noise. This is a delightful hotel and an excellent value.

Hotelier: M. Vergnault, 12 Rue Jean Goujon, 75008 Paris, Tel: 359.41.90, Telex: 643637, 42 Rooms, Expensive, Credit Cards: All Major

RESTAURANTS IN THE EIGHTH ARRONDISSEMENT

TAILLEVENT: A fabulous restaurant whose chef, Claude Deligne, supervises and maintains the excellence of the menu. The decor is very elegant, dressed with chandeliers, silver, crystal, linens and warmed by beautifully panelled walls.

15 Lamennais, 75008 Paris, Tel: 561.12.90, Closed Aug, No Credit Cards

LE BONAVENTURE: On the same quiet street as the Hotel San Regis, Le Bonaventure has a pleasing decor accented by original art. An outdoor courtyard is set with tables on balmy summer evenings and is very romantic surrounded by flowers and plants. Although the restaurant wasn't very busy in August, the food and presentation were excellent.

35 Rue Jean Goujon, 75008 Paris, Tel: 225.02.58, Credit Cards: AX, VS

REGENCE PLAZA: The Plaza Athenee is an elegant hotel and it has an elegant and superb restaurant. Even the most difficult to please have insisted that the Regence Plaza is one of the finest restaurants they've ever dined at.

25 Avenue Montaigne , 75008 Paris, Tel: 723.78.33,
Credit Cards: All Major

FOUQUETS: Behind Fouquet's sidewalk cafe is also a wonderful restaurant.

99 Rue Champs Elysees, 75008 Paris, Tel: 723.70.60,
Closed 15 Jul to 1 Sep, Credit Cards: All Major

LAUDEREE: Lauderee is the "in" place to gather for afternoon tea or a light lunch.   The pasteries are everything you would expect them to be in Paris and the "fashion show" is inevitable and entertaining.

on the Rue Royal, 75008 Paris

MAXIM's: Maxim's is not only an excellent restaurant but also a place to be seen, or rather, THE PLACE to be seen by the social set in Paris.   Very expensive.

3 Rue Royal, 75008 Paris, Tel: 265.27.94

TWELFTH ARRONDISSEMENT

RESTAURANTS IN THE TWELFTH ARRONDISSEMENT

LE TRAIN BLEU: Upstairs in the Gare de Lyon is the location of Le Train Bleu. Built for the exposition in 1900, the room is very ornate.   Tables are paired with comfortably padded seets, topped with polished, brass baggage racks; an old station clock dominates center stage.   The decor is reminiscent of an earlier era and the elegance and grandeur of first class travel.   The ceiling is a series of ornate paintings, each an exotic destination and banded in gold.   Although the food could not be considered gourmet, the menu offers a nice selection and the service and attention were exceptional. There is also a bar if you'd prefer just a drink.   This is a perfect rendezvous ... arrange a meeting after your arrival from Nice, (or stretch the romance a bit as we did, and arrive from the Gare de Lyon Metro).

20 Blvd Diderot, 75012 Paris, Tel: 343.09.06,
Credit Cards: AX, DC, VS

The SIXTEENTH ARRONDISSEMENT is Paris' elite residential district. It is a quiet area, characterized by stately elegant apartment buildings, lovely shopping streets and corner markets ... and by people who are always walking their dogs. The Rue de la Pompe and the Avenue Victor Hugo are two well-known avenues linked with beautiful and expensive shops. The Sixteenth Arrondissement is bordered on one side by the Bois de Boulogne, a scenic park where people walk, bicycle, run, play soccer and unwind.

HOTELS IN THE SIXTEENTH ARRONDISSEMENT

HOTEL ALEXANDER: Tucked between the elegant designer stores along the avenue Victor Hugo, the Hotel Alexander is highly spoken of by many who return time after time. The rooms are stylishly decorated and extremely comfortable. The entrance and sitting area are attractive. Popular with American travelers, English is spoken by all the employees.

102, Ave Victor Hugo, 75116 Paris, Tel: 553.64.65, Telex: 610373, 60 Rooms, Moderate, No Credit Cards

RESTAURANTS IN THE SIXTEENTH ARRONDISSEMENT

SAN FRANCISCO: San Francisco is said to have the best Italian food in Paris.

1, Rue Mirabeau, 75016 Paris, Tel: 647.75.44

Countryside Hotels

AGEN   Chateau Saint Marcel   Map# 59

Chateau de Saint Marcel, now under the supervision of Philippe Penche, was once the summer residence of the Count of Montesquieu. The castle, parts of which date back to the 13th century, has served in its various permutations as a hunting lodge and domicile for French nobility. The twelve bedrooms are comfortable and for the most part traditional in their decor. All the rooms are equipped with either bath or shower. Stone archways set the mood for the decor of the restaurant which is reminiscent of its earlier years and gatherings. Just five kilometers from Agen, the Chateau Saint Marcel enjoys a ten acre park and a restful river setting.

CHATEAU SAINT MARCEL
Owner & Manager: Philippe Penche
RN 113
Bon Encontre
47240 Agen
Tel: (53) 96.61.30
12 Rooms, Moderate
Open All Year
Credit Cards: VS, AX, DC, EC

AIX EN PROVENCE   Hotel Le Pigonnet   Map# 102

Aix is an intriguing city to explore. The beckoning cobble-stoned streets of the old quarter are particularly fun to wander at night and the illuminated tree-lined Boulevard Mirabeau is enchanting - a bit reminiscent of Paris with its many sidewalk cafes.   I have returned to Aix a number of times in search of a special hotel in the heart of the old section, but, without any success. However, it is just a fifteen minute walk to the very professionally run and attractive Hotel Le Pigonnet.   A tree-lined road leads you to this hotel that is away from the noise and traffic of the city.   Here you will find an abundance of flowers, cozy sitting rooms for daydreaming, a heated swimming pool, a fine restaurant and pleasant bedrooms.

HOTEL LE PIGONNET
Avenue du Pigonnet
13090 Aix en Provence
Tel: (42) 59.02.90 Telex: 410629
48 Rooms all with bath
Expensive
Open: All Year
Credit Cards: All Major
U.S. Rep: Trusthouse Forte
   Tel: (800) 223-5672 Telex: 236233
Bar, Terrace Restaurant, Pool

ALBI   Hostellerie Saint Antoine et La Reserve   Map# 71

Hostellerie Saint Antoine and La Reserve are actually two hotels owned and managed by the same family.   La Reserve is a new hotel, a mile and a half from Albi in the direction of Cordes.   The rooms, some of them modern and others with a rustic decor, are all attractively furnished.   There is a restaurant, a large pool, tennis courts and a lush green lawn separating the hotel from the river

Tarn.   Saint Antoine, which is moderately priced, has a garden and restaurant. Guests are welcome to use the pool and tennis facilities at La Reserve.

HOSTELLERIE SAINT ANTOINE ET LA RESERVE
Hotelier: M et Mme Rieux
Address: Route de Cordes, Fonvialane
81000 Albi
Tel: (63) 60.79.79 Telex: 520850
20 Rooms
Expensive
Credit Cards: All Major
Open April to November
U.S. Rep: David Mitchell
Tel: (212) 696-1323 Telex: 22123
Restaurant, Pool, Tennis

AMBOISE   Chateau de Pray   Map # 32

With its magnificent blue-grey turrets the Chateau de Pray dominates the hillside on the outskirts of Amboise.   Set regally in its own beautiful gardens, it would serve as a very appropriate choice of hotel while exploring the castles of the Loire Valley.   Monsieur and Mme Farard obviously love the hotel business and do everything possible to make their guests comfortable.   The rooms, which have a majestic feeling, are available on a demi-pension basis.   Dinner and breakfast are superb at a reasonable price.   You have the choice of service in your room, the breakfast room or on the garden terrace overlooking the Loire River.

CHATEAU DE PRAY
Hotelier: M A. Farard
Address: B.P. 146
37401 Amboise Cedex
Tel: (47) 57.23.67
16 Rooms, 14 with bath
Expensive
Credit Cards: All Major
Dates Open: 8 Feb to 31 Dec

ANDELYS, LES   Hotel La Chaine D'Or   Map# 6

Located in a village annex of Les Andelys the Hotel la Chaine D'Or looks up to the castle ruins and backs onto the Seine.   Just an hour or so to the north of Paris, Les Andelys is convenient to Charles De Gaulle Airport, Roissy and just a few miles from Giverney and Monet's home and gardens.   Restored in 1976 with funding mostly from individuals from the United States, a visit to Monet's home and the gardens that inspired his genious would prove a highlight of any trip. Depending on your itinerary, the Hotel La Chaine D'Or serves as a convenient overnight or dining choice.   Although the exterior needs a new coat of paint, the hotel benefits from unusually delightful management who strive to excell in service and attention to detail.   The Foucault Family take great pride in welcoming guests and overseeing details from the suggestion and selection of wine at dinner to the final decoration details and touches in the bedrooms.   Jean Claude was a baker in Paris before purchasing La Chaine D'Or and making a new home in Les Andelys.   Reason alone to overnight here would be to sample his breakfast croissants! Each year Monique attentively redecorates a few bedrooms. Soon all accommodations will achieve her desired standard and atmosphere. The bedrooms all enjoy views of the Seine and the constant, entertaining parade of barges. The hotel has two lovely restaurants. One is intimate, cozy and a delightful place for lunch. The service is relaxed and comfortable and the menu offers a limited but appealing selection of items. A larger room is a bit more formal in atmosphere. The dinner menu is excellent, the tables elegantly set and the service a bit more polished. From the windows of either restaurant you can look out to the Seine and a beautiful island and abandoned Manor.

HOTEL LA CHAINE D'OR
Jean Claude and Monique Foucault
27 Rue Grande
27700 Les Andelys
Tel: (32) 54.00.31
12 Rooms, 6 with bath
Inexpensive
Closed in January
Credit Cards: AX, CB

ANGOULEME (Hiersac)   Le Moulin du Maine Brun   Map # 46

This is an elegant hotel with a sophisticated atmosphere. The service is perfect. The rooms are beautiful. The location is extremely peaceful in comparison to the nearby city of Angouleme.

LE MOULIN DU MAINE BRUN
Hotelier: Famille Menager
Address: Asnieres sur Nouere
16290 Hiersac, (Charente)
Tel: (45) 96.92.62 Telex: 791053
20 Rooms
Moderate
Credit Cards: All Major
Open: Feb - Oct
U.S. Rep: David Mitchell
Tel: (212) 696-1323 Telex: 422123
Restaurant, Pool

ARLES   Hotel Jules Cesar   Map # 85

In the middle of the 17th century a Carmelite Convent was erected by Mother
Madeleine St. Joseph.   It was a residence for nuns until 1770 when the order was
expulsed in the midst of the French Revolution.   The convent then became state
property until it was purchased and transformed into a hotel in 1929.   In this
beautiful old convent, the Hotel Jules Cesar, a member of Relais de Campagne Et
Chateau Hotels has earned a rating of four stars under the directorship of
Monsieur Michel Albagnac.   The hotel is situated next to and shares a courtyard
with the Chapelle de la Charite.   The Chapel dates from the 17th century.
Rooms, for the most part, are large and spacious.   There are a few pretty
gardens, a courteous management and a good restaurant.   Room #72, on
the ground floor, with windows opening onto the garden, is the choice room.
Two large double beds are in this massive, but elegant chamber.

HOTEL JULES CESAR
Hotelier: Michael Albagnac
Address: B.P. 116, Blvd. des Lices
13631 Arles, (B. du R.)
Tel: (90) 93.43.20 Telex: 400239
62 Rooms, All with bath or shower
Expensive
Credit Cards: All Major
U.S. Rep: David Mitchell
Tel: (212) 696-1323 Telex: 422123
Open All Year

ARLES   Hotel D'Arlatan   Map# 85

HOTEL D'ARLATAN
Monsieur et Madame Roger Desjardin
26 rue du Sauvage
13631 Arles, (B. du R.)
Tel: (90) 93.56.66 Telex: 441203
46 Rooms, 42 with bath
Moderate
Open All Year
Credit Cards: All Major

Found tucked off of one of the small streets in the center of Arles, near the Place du Forum, within easy walking distance to everything, the Hotel D'Arlatan is a quaint hotel ornamented with antiques.   In the 12th, 15th and 17th centuries it belonged to the Counts d'Arlatan de Beaumont and served as their private home.   It is now the pride of Monsieur et Madame Roger Desjardin and they offer you an ideal retreat with charming accommodations and service.   The hotel also has a pretty and peaceful inner patio with a courtyard.

AUDRIEU   Chateau d'Audrieu   Map# 13

The Chateau D'Audrieu affords the countryside traveller luxurious accommodations within the walls of a beautiful 18th century chateau.   Its own expanse of grounds provide a parkland setting and a pool which is a welcome treat on warm summer days.   All twenty-two bedrooms, four of which are commodious suites, are furnished in elegant antiques and have private bathrooms.

CHATEAU D'AUDRIEU
Hotelier: M et Mme Livry-Level
Address: Audrieu, 14250 Tilly sur Seulles
Tel: (31) 80.21.52
19 Rooms, 3 Apartments
Expensive, Credit Cards: AX, VS
Open Mar to Nov, Pool
U.S. Rep: David Mitchell
Tel: (212) 696-1323 Telex: 422123

Of all the Hotel de la Postes in France, this particular one in Avallon is perhaps the most famous and definitely ranks number one with gourmets.   Once an old mail stop, it also is interesting to note that Napoleon stopped here in 1813 on his return from Elba.   Dining is, of course, superb and rooms are alluringly restful.

HOSTELLERIE DE LA POSTE
Hotelier: M et Mme Rene Hure
Address: 13 Place Vauban,
89200 Avallon
Tel: (86) 34.06.12 telex: 800997
26 Rooms, 25 with private bath
Expensive
Open January through November
Credit Cards: AX, VS, DC
U.S. Rep: David Mitchell
Tel: (212) 696-1323 Telex: 422123

Moulin des Ruats is a charming, wood-shingled cottage surrounded by greenery. An old wheat mill, it was transformed into a hotel in 1914 and has been managed by the same family since 1926.   Monsieur et Mme Luciani make a point to satisfy your desire to sample excellent French cuisine.   The twenty rooms are quite simple in their decor but pleasant and reasonable in price.   The setting either in the garden or in the cozy restaurant makes for an intimate dinner.

HOSTELLERIE MOULIN DES RUATS
Monsieur et Madame Luciani
Vallee du Cousin
89200 Avallon
Tel: (86) 34.07.14
21 Rooms, 14 with private bath
Inexpensive, Credit Cards: VS, AX
Open March through October
U.S. Rep: David Mitchell
Tel: (212) 696-1323 Telex: 422123

AVIGNON   Hotel d'Europe   Map # 91

Hotel d'Europe is a beautiful eighteenth century mansion formerly the home of the Marquis of Gravezon. You leave the busy street by passing under an arched entry and arrive in a peaceful garden with tables and chairs directly in front of the hotel. The rooms vary in size, but they are all comfortable and decorated with eighteenth century furniture. There are two large suites: room #1 and #2. Room #2 is the nicer because it also has a large fireplace. Tapestries cover many of the floors and walls, which add warmth and loveliness. The hotel has a fine restaurant, the Vieille Fontaine, and bar.

HOTEL D'EUROPE
Hotelier: P. Joubert
Address: 12, Place Crillon
84000 Avignon, (Vaucluse)
Tel: (90) 82.66.92 telex: 431965
64 Rooms, 6 Apartments
Moderate
Open All Year
U.S. Rep: Jacques de Larsay
Tel: (800) 223-1510

BAGNOLS SUR CEZE   Chateau de Coulorgues   Map# 94

This lovely old "provencial" chateau has an atmosphere of yesterday with comforts of today. The rooms are nicely decorated. I recommend the restaurant. The tennis courts and swimming pool are a plus for sport lovers.

CHATEAU DE COULORGUES
Address: Route d'Avignon
30200 Bagnols sur Ceze
Tel: (66) 89.52.78
23 Rooms
Moderate
Closed in February
Restaurant, Tennis, Pool

Hotel La Cardinal is a romantic old home on the Rhone River.   Ivy-clad and shuttered, La Cardinale is surrounded by its own beautiful acreage and has a lovely swimming pool.   With a history that dates back to the 17th century it is handsomely furnished with traditional pieces.   Cuisine, as the region suggests, is excellent.   The bedrooms are beautifully appointed and inviting.

LA CARDINALE ET SA RESIDENCE
Hotelier: Mme M. Motte
Address: Baix, 07210 Chomerac
Tel (75) 85.80.40
17 Rooms, all with private bath
Expensive, Credit Cards: All Major
Open: 16 February to 3 January
U.S. Rep: David Mitchell
Tel: (212) 696-1323 Telex: 422123
Swimming Pool

Barbizon has attracted artists for ages and the charming, yet elegant Hostellerie du Bas Breau has had its share of famous guests.   The most renown guest was Robert Louis Stevenson, who spent much time here, due to health and also because of his deep love for this small town in the corner of the forest of Fontainebleau.   The hotel, also called "Stevenson's House",   has twenty rooms in newer wings behind the entry. Each is different, yet has a lovely bathroom; is luxurious and in an old decor. The restaurant is superb and attracts guests in the evening away from some of the finest Paris establishments! With unusually attractive flower arrangements on each table, the atmosphere is elegant and romantic.

HOSTELLERIE DU BAS-BREAU
Hotelier: M Fava
Address: 77630 Barbizon
Tel: (6) 066.40.05 Telex: 690953
12 Rooms, 7 Apartments
Expensive, Credit Cards: All Major
Open mid-Feb through December
U.S. Rep: David Mitchell
Tel: (212) 696-1323 Telex: 422123

BARBOTAN   **Thermal et sa Bastide Gasconne**   **Map# 61**

HOTEL THERMAL ET SA BASTIDE GASCONNE
Hotelier: Hubert Dayon
Address: Barbotan les Thermes
32150 Cazaubon, (Gers)
Tel: (62) 09.52.09 telex: 521009
47 Rooms, Moderate, Credit Cards: AX
Open: 1 April to 31 October
U.S. Rep: David Mitchell
Tel: (212) 696-1323 Telex: 422123

Hotel Gasconne is an eighteenth century Bastide with luxurious accommodations. It is set in a region of thermal spas, where health and dining are refined concerns. Swimming pool, and tennis facilities are available.

LES BAUX EN PROVENCE   L'Oustau Baumaniere   Map# 86

It is known to me through personal experience and the praise of fellow travelers that this is a marvelous hotel.   There are gardens for strollers; a beautiful pool; magnificent bedrooms; superb service.   The atmosphere and furnishings are rich in antiques and tradition.   The restaurant serves exceptional cuisine. However, my most recent visit to L'Oustau Baumaniere was at the lunch hour and I would like to assume that the hurried reception and untidy public bathrooms were a result of the afternoon crowd and not a change in the professional and high standard of service both expected and associated with the hotel.

L'OUSTAU BAUMANIERE
Hotelier: M Thuillier
Address: dans le Vallon
13520 Les Baux en Provence
Tel: (90) 97.33.07 telex: 420203
15 Rooms
Expensive
Open: 1 Mar to 15 Jan
Credit Cards: AE, DC, EC, VS
U.S. Rep: David Mitchell
Tel: (212) 696-1323 telex: 422123
Pool

Set in the shadow of the enchanting village of Les Baux en Provence, La Cabro D'Or is directly associated with L'Oustau Baumaniere. It is, however, a simpler version (which is reflected in the prices) of the same hotel. Set in an expanse of unusually beautiful grounds, La Cabro d'Or is lovely and the children will enjoy feeding the swans and ducks with crumbs from the morning croissants!

LA CABRO D'OR
Hotelier: M Mascoloni
Address: dans le Vallon
13520 Les Baux en Provence
Tel: (90) 97.33.21 telex: 401810
19 Rooms
Moderate
Open: 21 Dec to 14 Nov
Credit Cards: All Major
U.S. Rep: David Mitchell
Tel: (212) 696-1323 telex: 422123
Tennis

It was such a change, when rather than walk up to a reception desk I rang the doorbell of the Auberge de la Benvengudo and home of the Beaupieds. The rooms are attractive and pleasant. One is forced to eat a delicious dinner in the adorable restaurant, (demi-pension obligatory)! The hotel has a lovely, refreshing pool and a large yard filled with trees and colorful flowers.

AUBERGE DE LA BENVENGUDO
Hotelier: M et Mme Daniel Beaupied
Address: 13520 Les Baux en Provence
Tel: (90) 97.32.50
16 Rooms
Moderate
Open: 1 Feb to 1 Nov

BEAUGENCY   Hostellerie de la Tonnellerie   Map# 36

Renovated from a wine-merchant's house in the little village of Tavers near the medieval town of Beaugency, La Tonnellerie has been a hotel for thirteen years. In the heart of the Chateau Region, the Hostellerie is excellent because of its location and its accommodations. The restaurant is situated at the very place where, a century ago, coppers made barrels for the wine merchants. The menu boasts a number of regional specialties. Enhanced by lots of antiques the decor throughout is charming and each room personalized. Truly a lovely hotel where your welcome is assured by the owners themselves.

HOSTELLERIE DE LA TONNELLERIE
Hotelier: M et Mme Aulagnon
Address: 12, rue des Eaux-Bleues
Tavers, 45190 Beaugency
Tel: (38) 44.68.15
27 Rooms all with private bath
Moderate
Open: Easter to 30 September
Credit Cards: DC
Swimming Pool

BEAULIEU   Hotel La Reserve   Map# 111

Described by Monsieur Henri Maria, perhaps one of the most gracious and hospitable directeurs I've met in my travels through France, La Reserve is a "restaurant avec chambres".   It is then perhaps the most luxurious "restaurant with rooms" in France!   The restaurant was founded by the Lottier family in 1894 on the same spot that it occupies today.   Its reputation as one of France's most accredited restaurants is now almost a tradition and acknowledged by celebrities and royalty from its earliest beginnings. You will be expertly catered to both in the dining room and hotel.   One can dine in a very elegant restaurant with floor to ceiling windows overlooking the salt-water pool and ocean, bordered by an outside terrace used for lunch and dinner in the balmy summer months.   There are also two small dining rooms on each wing that can be reserved for private functions. One opens onto the terrace and would make an ideal setting for any special occasion.   The pool is filled with sea water , heated in the winter, is surrounded by a private dock where private parties station while dining at La Reserve.

Guests not only return year after year to La Reserve, but request the same room. There are fifty bedrooms in all, each traditionally furnished and the three apartments have a sitting room and private balcony.

HOTEL LA RESERVE
Director: Henri Maria
5, Blvd General Leclerc
06310 Beaulieu sur Mer
Tel: (93) 01.00.01, telex: 470301
50 Rooms, 3 Apartments
Very Expensive
Closed 1 Dec until 10 Jan
Credit Cards: All Major
U.S. Rep: David Mitchell
Tel: (212) 696-1323 telex: 422123

BEAUNE   Hotel de la Poste   Map # 129

Although, sometimes a bit noisy, there are advantages to staying in a town which is both the capital and at the heart of the Cote D'Or wine region.   Beaune has an architecturally unique Hotel de Ville, an interesting wine museum and with the town as a base, you can easily venture out to explore and sample some of the world's finest wines.   The Hotel de la Poste is a lovely hotel with a dedicated management and delightful restaurant. Here you can spend a memorable vacation with a touch of luxury.

HOTEL DE LA POSTE
Hotelier: M Chevillot
Address: 1, blvd Clemenceau
21200 Beaune, (Cote d'Or)
Tel: (80) 22.08.11
21 Rooms, Expensive
Open: 1 Apr to 19 Nov
Credit Cards: All Major
U.S. Rep: Jacques de Larsay
Tel: (800) 223-1510

BEAUNE   Hotel Le Cep   Map# 129

At the center of the dear town of Beaune, Le Cep offers cozy rooms and
attentive service. The hotel has beamed ceilings, a winding staircase which
creaks, and a great deal of charm.   There is no formal restaurant, but often,
with advance notice, the Falces will have a light meal prepared for you.

HOTEL LE CEP
Hotelier: M et Mme Falce
Address: 27, Rue Maufaux
21200 Beaune, (Cote d'Or)
Tel: (80) 22.35.48
21 Rooms, Moderate
Open: 15 Mar to 30 Nov
Credit Cards: All Major

This was once the home of Mounet Sully, the famous 19th century actor.   One of the dining rooms was his private theater.   The apartment, with its magnificent bed and hand painted walls, directly above, was his bedroom, reputedly visited by Sarah Bernhardt.   The courtyard columns were individually designed by leading artists of his time.   The majority of rooms are found in the other wing and, although attractive, were not well heated in early November.   However, the owners have changed in recent years and although, I did not have an opportunity to revisit it, readers have informed me of the dramatic improvement in management.

CHATEAU HOTEL MOUNET SULLY
Hotelier: Christian Lonvaud
Address: Route de Mussidan
24100 Bergerac, (Dordogne)
Tel: (53) 57.04.21
8 Rooms
Inexpensive
Open: 15 Dec to 14 Nov
Credit Cards: AE, DC

BEYNAC ET CAZENAC   Hotel Bonnet   Map# 55

Soon after the publication of the first edition of FRENCH COUNTRY INNS AND CHATEAU HOTELS I was directed to the Hotel Bonnet and have since returned for repeated visits.   Serenely located on the bend of the Dordogne, in the shadow of the impressive Chateau de Beynac, the Bonnet is indeed a "gem". The rooms are simple in decor, but the restaurant setting, either indoors with large windows exposing a serene river panorama or on the vine-covered terrace, encourages one to linger for hours. The menu is superb and the gracious Bonnet Family has managed this inn for almost a century. The welcome is genuine.

HOTEL BONNET
Hotelier: Famille Bonnet
Address: Beynac et Cazenac
24220 St. Cyprien (Dordogne)
Tel: (53) 29.50.01
22 Rooms
Inexpensive
Open: 1 April 15 October

LES BEZARDS   Auberge les Templiers   Map# 143

An hour south of Paris, L'Auberge les Templiers provides a wonderful retreat. The hotel is relatively new, but the furniture, of wood-timbered design and rooms decorated with warm and colorful fabrics, hides that fact well. The modern bathroom facilities and the large pool are the only "give-aways." Whether your reasons for coming to the Auberge are for business, a quiet weekend away from the city, a night's stopover, or understandably for its charm, it will prove to be a good choice.

AUBERGE LES TEMPLIERS
Address: Les Bezards
45290 Nogent sur Vernisson
Tel: (38) 31.80.01 telex: 780998
22 Rooms, Moderate
Open: 15 February to 14 January
Credit Cards: All Major
U.S. Rep: David Mitchell
Tel: (212) 696-1323 telex: 422123

LES BEZARDS   Chateau des Bezards   Map# 143

Chateau les Bezards stands grandly not far from the road leading to Paris. The massive entry has a medieval appearance. The chateau has a high ceiling, big comfortable chairs and a blazing fire to read by. The dining room is beautifully paneled, with fabrics of green and red accenting the wood. The rooms vary in decor and are all comfortable and attractive. If you find you cannot resist the cuisine a pool, an (indoor) sauna, an exercise/recreation room will help remove some extra pounds.

CHATEAU DES BEZARDS
Address: Les Bezards
45290 Nogent sur Vernisson
Tel: (38) 31.80.03 telex: 780335
38 Rooms, Moderate
Credit Cards: All Major
Swimming Pool, Park, Tennis

I was absolutely charmed by Le Prieure as a result of both the owner and the enchanting decor of the inn.   I was surprised to discover a hotel of such superior quality tucked away in the small hillside village of Bonnieux ...   until I learned that Monsieur Chapotin is a member of a family long responsible for some of France's finest and most prestigious hotels.   Recently leaving a career of finance behind in Paris, Monsieur Chapotin has chosen a small 17th century catholic abbey as his new venture and second home.   You will discover incredible antiques, some original to the Meurice in Paris, removed before his family sold the hotel, some cherished heirlooms, in a setting of luxurious calm. Le Prieure has a superb restaurant with specialties all impossible to resist.   A list to tempt even the most disciplined: Foie gras frais de canard; Canard aux olives de Nyons; Saumon a l'oseille; Truite marinee au vinaigre; Gateau au chocolat!   The restaurant is gorgeous with soft, pale pink table cloths, fresh flowers, soft lighting.   On warmer evenings meals are served in the shade of the garden.   The traditionally beautiful bedrooms are excellent in the choice and enhancement of decor.   It is hard not to take special notice of the magnificent pieces of art and paintings found throughout the inn.   I soon understood the extent and appreciation Monsieur Chapotin has for art.   He graciously extended an invitation to attend a showing at a local gallery and also learned of his plans to turn the adjoining chapel into a gallery.   Under the care and direction of Monsieur Chapotin and Charlotte Keller, Le Prieure is outstanding.

HOSTELLERIE LE PRIEURE
Remy Chapotin, Charlotte Keller
84480 Bonnieux
Tel: (90) 75.80.78
10 Rooms
Moderate
Open 15 Feb to 15 Nov

BOURDEILLES   Hotel des Griffons   Map# 50

In searching for an ideal luncheon spot when escorting my very first group to France, I was thrilled to discover the enchanting village of Bourdeilles and the marvelous Hotel Des Griffons.   Wanting only the very best for my group, I was perhaps a bit difficult to please, but the charms of the Hotel Des Griffons met and surpassed my every demand and expectation.   Crowned by its castle, the village creeks with age, but clinging to a narrow bridge, this hotel shelters ten cozy bedrooms, beautiful modern bathrooms, and a restaurant where Madame Denise Deborde supervises your care and personally pampers and tempts your palate.   Longing to linger, I eagerly returned with my next group, and expanded our luncheon spot into a two-day stay.

HOTEL DES GRIFFONS
Hotelier: Madame Denise Deborde
Address: Bourdeilles
24310 Brantome, (Dordogne)
Tel: (53) 05.75.61
10 Rooms, Inexpensive
Open: 1 Mar to 30 Sept
Credit Cards: VS, DC, MC

BRANTOME   Hostellerie le Moulin de l'Abbaye   Map# 49

With its architecturally interesting Benedictine Abbey, lovely gray-stone homes, peaceful expanses of green, and narrow streets transected by and following the course of the River Dronne, Brantome commands the visit of many. Enhancing the charms of this village is the Hostellerie Le Moulin de L'Abbaye. From its own quiet setting, straddling the Dronne, the inn looks across the span of water at Brantome.   Eight romantic bedrooms, beautifully appointed, and an elegant restaurant all enjoy and profit from this idyllic setting.

HOSTELLERIE LE MOULIN DE L'ABBAYE
Hotelier: Regis et Catherine Bulot
Address: 24310 Brantome, (Dordogne)
Tel: (53) 05.80.22 telex: 560570
9 Rooms, Expensive
Open 15 May to 7 October
Credit Cards: All Major

Le Lot is overwhelming in its beauty and the splendor of its towns.   I was truly stunned and a bit fearful of not being able to find an inn to equal its glory.   Le Lot warrants an outstanding hotel and La Pescalerie would do justice to any region.   Located just over 2km outside the village of Cabrerets, (famous for the Grotto du Perche Merle), the family home of Monsieur Belcour is remarkably beautiful.   La Pescalerie is a magnificent weathered-stone manor house in a lovely riverside setting with the tranquil Lot Valley as its backdrop.   Ten handsomely appointed bedrooms are divided between two levels and open onto the garden through thick 16th and 17th century walls.   The rooms are pleasingly different, yet, each an attractive melange of modern and cherished antiques. The top floor rooms are set under the beams of the house with delightful dormer windows and a few have a loft ideal for children with a sense of adventure. Opened only five years ago,   La Pescalerie ideally accommodates those who have the time to linger in the magnificent Lot Valley.   It has a lovely bar and an elegant restaurant.

LA PESCALERIE
Hotelier: Helene Combette
Address: 46330 Cabrerets (Lot)
Tel: (65) 31.22.55
10 Rooms, Moderate
Open April to November
Credit Cards: AX, VS, DC
U.S. Rep: David Mitchell
Tel: (212) 696-1323 telex: 422123

You feel as if you have entered the middle ages as you head up the narrow, winding cobble-stoned streets to the Chateau Grimaldi.   You pass little shops, homes with flowers on their window ledges, and even smaller streets leading down to mysterious places.   As the streets become narrower, you pass under buildings which form an archway above and then arrive at the hotel, Le Cagnard. The hotel enables you to remain in a medieval setting, rather than become a part of the bustling life offered by the Cote D'Azur.   The Cagnard has been in operation for 40 years.   M and Mme Barel make a guest feel welcome and at home. Dinner on the terrace, set under a full moon, is a romantic experience and the presentation of the cuisine is exceptional.   The elevator is charming, biblical paintings change with each floor, and I found some marvelous rooms and views. Rooms numbered 2 through 12 have a medieval flavor; there are also some lovely modern apartments.

LE CAGNARD
Hotelier: M et Mme Barel
Address: Rue Pontis Long
06800 Cagnes sur Mer,
(Haut de Cagnes)
Tel: (93) 20.73.21
19 Rooms, Expensive
Open: 18 Dec to 31 Oct
Credit Cards: All Major
U.S. Rep: David Mitchell
Tel: (212) 696-1323 telex: 422123

This hotel, resembling a Normandy farm, is located in the heart of the country. Local residents gather here for Sunday dinners to enjoy the excellence of the food.   The rooms are elegant and quiet, and provide a relaxing environment. Accommodations are accepted on a demi-pension basis only.

LE PETIT COQ AUX CHAMPS
Hotelier: M Pommier
Address: Domaine de la Pommeraye
Campigny, 27500 Pont Audemer
Tel: (32) 41.04.19
10 Rooms, Moderate
Open: 1 Mar to 1 Dec
Credit Cards: All Major

CARCASSONNE   Hotel de la Cite   Map# 67

Explore the medieval fortress of Carcassonne and then settle for an evening secure behind its massive walls in the intimate Hotel De La Cite.   Recessed into the walls near the Bascilica St. Nazaire, many of the bedrooms open up onto the ramparts and a small enclosed garden.   The hotel is on the site of the ancient episcopal palace and offers you the refined comfort of its rooms in a medieval atmosphere.   Nicely decorated, the rooms vary in price according to size and view.

HOTEL DE LA CITE
Hotelier: Dominique Lasserre
Address: Place St. Nazaire
11000 Carcassonne, (Aude)
Tel: (68) 25.03.34 telex: 500829
54 Rooms, Expensive
Open: April to October
Credit Cards: AE, CB, DC
U.S. Rep: Jacques de Larsay
Tel: (800) 223-1510

CARCASSONNE   Domaine d'Auriac   Map # 67

Domaine d'Auriac is a lovely ivy clad manor on the outskirts of Carcassonne. Elegant, the rooms are nicely furnished and all are with bath.   The restaurant, overlooking the pool and garden, is quite attractive.   The bar, located in the old wine cellar, is quaint.   The management is responsible for personal touches and professional service. Enjoy the pool, tennis and park.

DOMAINE D'AURIAC
Hotelier: M et Mme B. Rigaudis
Address: Rte Saint Hilaire, BP 554
11000 Carcassonne, (Aude)
Tel: (68) 25.75.22 telex: 500385
23 Rooms, Expensive
Open: 1 February to 15 January
Credit Cards: All Major
U.S. Rep: David Mitchell
Tel: (212) 696-1323 telex: 422123

CASTILLON DU GARD   Le Vieux Castillon   Map # 82

At the heart of an authentic medieval village, just three miles from the architecturally splendid Pont Du Gard, Le Vieux Castillon has thirty-five bedrooms and two luxurious suites.   On a knoll surrounded by the gray-green olive trees and stretches of vineyards, the Vieux Castillon is an enchanting town of red tile, sun-washed houses, so typical of Provence.   It serves as an ideal location for exploring the region.   The restaurant offers an excellent selection of local cuisine and specialties.   While here, experience the flavor of Provence and a truly lovely hotel.

LE VIEUX CASTILLON
Hotelier: Roger Traversac
Tel: (66) 37.00.77 telex: 490946
35 Rooms, Expensive
Open: 10 March to 31 December
Credit cards: VS, BC
U.S. Rep: David Mitchell
Tel: (212) 696-1323 telex: 422123
Tennis, Pool

CAUDEBEC EN CAUX   Manoir de Retival   Map # 11

Manoir de Retival is an old hunting lodge, just outside of town and on the river's edge.   The staff is under the direction of the very gracious Mme Collett.   The rooms vary greatly.   A few were marvelous, while others were rather seedy. Some of the nicer rooms within the main building are: La Directrice, a large room overlooking the river; La Grise (also with its own private bath); La Rose a bit smaller, and very feminine. In the annex there are four rooms; only one of which I would recommend: La Lavande. The lovely restaurant will captivate you with its large fireplace and beautiful wood beams and paneling. The hotel does not have a restaurant.

MANOIR DE RETIVAL
Hotelier: Mme Collett
Address: Rue St Clair
76490 Caudebec en Caux
Tel: (35) 96.11.22
10 Rooms, Moderate
Open: 30 Mar to 02 Nov
Credit Cards: AX, DC

CHAGNY   Hotel Lameloise   Map # 128

Hotel Lameloise is named after the remarkable family who owns it. The rooms are all carefully decorated with a touch of elegance. The restaurant, famous for its marvelous cuisine, is delightfully intimate.

HOTEL LAMELOISE
Hotelier: Lameloise Family
Address: Place d'Armes
71150 Chagny, (S. et L.)
Tel: (85) 87.08.85
25 Rooms, Moderate
Closed for part of July & Dec
Credit Cards: Visa
U.S. Rep: David Mitchell
Tel: (212) 696-1323 telex: 422123

| CHAMBORD | Hostellerie Saint Michel | Map# 35 |

Hostellerie St. Michel is located opposite the Chateau de Chambord, not more than two hundred yards away. The rooms are plain but comfortable. A few (Rooms 7, 5 and 1) have unobstructed views of the chateau. Room 7, a corner room, is the largest of the three. Make a point of meeting the charming owner, which will not be difficult since she is most interested in the activities of her guests.

HOSTELLERIE SAINT MICHEL
Address: Chambord, 41250 Bracieux
Tel: (54) 20.31.31
38 Rooms, Inexpensive
Open: 22 December to 12 November
Credit Cards: Visa

Le Moulin du Roc is a small seventeenth and eighteenth century stone mill. The eight rooms, although not large, are each stunning. The bathrooms are all modern. One apartment is particularly enchanting. It has an adjoining, small room with a single bed, and a large room with a marvelous wood canopy double bed. Windows from the room overlook the lazy Drome River, the gardens, and the beautiful birch lined pastures. The dining room is small and captivating. Madame Gardillou is responsible for the kitchen and the cuisine is exquisite. Monsieur Gardillou serves as a most gracious and charming host. Le Moulin du Roc remains a favorite, year after year!

LE MOULIN DU ROC
Hotelier: M et Mme Gardillou
Address: 24530 Champagnac de Belair
Tel: (53) 54.80.36
8 Rooms, Moderate
Closed: 15 Nov-15 Dec & 15 Jan-15 Mar
Credit Cards: All Major
U.S. Rep: David Mitchell
Tel: (212) 696-1323 telex: 422123

CHAMPILLON   Royal Champagne   Map # 139

In the heart of champagne country, you may enjoy an excellent meal at Royal Champagne, and taste some classic champagnes. Famous for its cuisine, Royal Champagne also has twenty-two attractive rooms. They are not exceptionally large and vary only in the color of the wallpaper, but they all have baths and small private terraces overlooking the vineyards.

ROYAL CHAMPAGNE
Hotelier: M Dellinger
Address: Champillon, 51160 Ay
Tel: (26) 51.11.51
22 Rooms, Expensive
Open: All Year
Credit Cards: All Major
U.S. Rep: David Mitchell
Tel: (212) 696-1323 telex: 422123

CHATEAU-ARNOUX	La Bonne Etape	Map# 106

I am still not certain how I could possibly have overlooked this marvelous hotel during my first countryside explorations and research. La Bonne Etape, a pastel-wash manor house with its tiled roof, is beautifully suited for the region of Haute Provence. The hotel has eleven bedrooms and seven apartments, all attractively decorated and a quality restaurant. The gracious Famille Gleize provide the service and attention.

LA BONNE ETAPE
Hotelier: Pierre et Jany Gleize
Address: 04160 Chateau-Arnoux
Tel: (92) 64.00.09 telex: 430605
18 Rooms, Moderate
Open: 02 Feb-19 Nov & 25 Nov-03 Jan
Credit Cards: All Major

CHATEAUNEUF DU PAPE   Hostellerie Fines Roches   Map # 93

It seems only appropriate that in a region of France's finest wines is also the location of a superior chateau-hotel and outstanding restaurant. With an imposing position on a hillside exposed only to vineyards, the Hostellerie Fines Roches has surprisingly few rooms. The seven suites are handsomely furnished, spacious, and attentively equipped with any convenience you might desire. Monsieur Estevenin is a gracious host to some very famous clientele and acknowledges their preference for privacy and quiet. Although he still oversees the kitchen, his son is in charge as the chef. Some specialities include: Filets de rougets and a magnificent assortment of desserts. Monsieur Estevenin is rightly very proud of his son's capabilities, has gladly relinquished the duties, and his time is now spent perfecting a welcome that is as unusual as the hotel itself.

HOSTELLERIE FINES ROCHES
Hotelier: Henri Estevenin
84230 Chateauneuf du Pape
tel: (90) 83.70.23
7 Rooms, Expensive
Closed Christmas to Feb

CHATILLON SUR SEINE   Hotel de la Cote D'Or   Map# 146

"Qu'il est doux de ne rien faire...", expect to relax and enjoy yourself, at the hotel de la Cote D'Or.   An attractive young couple, M and Mme Richard, own and run the hotel.   There are twelve rooms of comfortable size, half with bath. Each has been carefully decorated by Mme Richard, who continues to add touches and improvements each year.   The restaurant is charming, and in the warmer months meals are served in the garden.

HOTEL COTE D'OR
Hotelier: M et Mme Richard
Address: Rue Ronot
21400 Chatillon sur Seine
Tel: (80) 91.13.29
10 Rooms, Moderate
Closed in January
Credit Cards: AX, VS, DC

Hotel Descriptions   167

Chateau de Chaumontel is a marvelous hotel that once belonged to the family of the Prince de Conde.   The moment you cross the moat and enter the grounds of this breath-taking chateau, you will be tempted to extend your reservations. On a cushion of virgin snow or framed by colorful trees, Chateau de Chaumontel is striking and beautiful.   A wonderful staff and accommodations will add to your vacation's romantic setting.

CHATEAU DE CHAUMONTEL
Hotelier: M Bondon
Address: 21 Rue Andre Vassord
Chaumontel, 95270 Luzarches
Tel: (3) 471.00.30
20 Rooms, 17 with private bath
Moderate
Closed: 16 July-25 August
25 km from Charles de Gaulle

Opposite the gates that open to the road winding to the Chateau de Chaumont, you will discover a lovely hotel where you will want to linger.   You will be charmed by the wood beamed interior, the glowing fire, the beautiful dining room, quaint salons and Mrs. Bonnigal's hospitality.   The rooms are in warm and attractive colors, the furniture is beautiful and the bathrooms are modern and spacious. Splurge, as the best rooms are the most expensive.

HOSTELLERIE DU CHATEAU
Proprietor: M Bonnigal
Hotelier: Me Desmadryl
Address: Chaumont sur Loire
41550 Onzain
Tel: (54) 20.98.04
15 Rooms, Moderate
Open 01 March to 01 November
Credit Cards: VS, DC
U.S. Rep: Jacques de Larsay
Tel: (800) 223-1510

CHEFFES   **Chateau de Teildras**   **Map# 27**

Located between Brittany and the Loire Valley, the Chateau De Teildras welcomes you to a serene pastoral setting.   Owned and managed by the Comte and Comtesse de Bernard du Breil, the chateau has eleven beautifully appointed bedrooms and   a restaurant featuring the excellent regional specialities. The hotel is surrounded by twenty-five hectares and it affords some exceptional horseback riding.

CHATEAU DE TEILDRAS
Hotelier: Comte de Bernard du Breil
Address: Cheffes
49330 Chateauneuf sur Sarthe
Tel: (41) 42.61.08
11 Rooms, Moderate
Open: 15 March-15 November
Credit Cards: AE, VS, DC
U.S. Rep: David Mitchell
Tel: (212) 696-1323 telex: 422123

CHENEHUTTE LES TUFFEAUX   Le Prieure   Map# 28

Le Prieure, at Chenehutte les Tuffeaux, is a first class hotel with a fantastic forty mile panoramic view of the Loire.   Here they seem to have forgotten that the days of nobility are past, for all guests are treated as if they were kings and queens.

LE PRIEURE
Hotelier: Mme Bernard
Address: Chenehutte les Tuffeaux
49350 Gennes
Tel: (41) 50.15.31 telex: 720379
36 Rooms, Expensive
Open: 6 March to 4 January
Credit Cards: AX
U.S. Rep: David Mitchell
Tel(212) 696-1323 telex: 422123

This lovely, small hotel is very near the Chateau de Chenonceaux.   Here you may linger over the charm of the most elegant of renaissance chateaux in the Loire Valley.   A friendly welcome to guests has been a tradition in the Jeudi family for generations.   The gastronomic splendors of their table and the comfort of their rooms will convince you that they know how to provide the delights you have been longing for and will not forget.

BON LABOUREUR ET DU CHATEAU
Hotelier: Jeudi Family
Address: 37150 Chenonceaux
Tel: (47) 29.90.02
29 Rooms, Inexpensive
Open: April to November
Credit Cards: AX, VS, DC

Once a mill, this ivy-covered hotel is situated along a river and downstream from an old stone bridge.   There are twelve rooms, nothing exceptional, but they are comfortable, clean and have modern bathroom facilities.   Three kilometers from the mill is the Relais de Surone, an annex, that is very old and quiet. The hotel's restaurant is tempting   and meals are served outside during the summer months.   You sit on a terrace overlooking the water, shaded by trees, and enjoy a drink at white rod-iron tables.

MOULIN DE VEY
Hotelier: Mme Leduc
Address: 14570 Clecy le Vey
Tel: (31) 69.71.08
12 Rooms in the Mill
6 Rooms in the Relais Surone
Inexpensive, Credit Cards: AX, DC
Open: All Year

COGNAC   Moulin de Cierzac   Map# 47

Just fourteen kilometers from Cognac in a decidedly prestigious wine region, the Moulin de Cierzac invites you to a peaceful setting where both the regional cuisine and drinks may be sampled and enjoyed. The hotel itself is in a renovated 17th century mill and all the bedrooms are cheerfully decorated.

MOULIN DE CIERZAC
Hotelier: Patrick Labouly
Address: Cognac, BP2
16660 Saint Fort Sur le Ne
Tel: (45) 83.61.32
10 Rooms, Moderate
Open: All Year
Credit Cards: VS, CB

COLROY LA ROCHE   Hostellerie la Cheneaudiere   Map# 136

Colroy la Roche is a town, typical of the Alsacian region.   On the hillside, overlooking the town and surrounding valleys and forests, is the Hostellerie La Cheneaudiere.   It was built to resemble a country tavern.   The rooms are lovely and are identical in style.   All are with bath, telephone, television, and minibar.   Upon arrival at the hotel I recognized many of the parked cars as ones which had passed me earlier on the road, so this is apparently a popular spot in the region.

HOSTELLERIE LA CHENEAUDIERE
Hotelier: M et Mme Francois
Address: 67420 Colroy la Roche
Tel: (88) 97.61.64 telex: 870438
28 Rooms, Moderate
Open: March til December
Credit Cards: All Major
U.S. Rep: David Mitchell
Tel: (212) 696-1323 telex: 422123

CONCARNEAU   Hotel La Belle Etoile   Map# 20

Hotel La Belle Etoile is an expensive but elegant hotel that is situated on the the southern coast of Brittany looking out to the sheltered bay of the Cabellou. From the hotel it   is just a short walk down to a fine sandy beach.   La Belle

Etoile has its own private mooring should you decide to arrive by yacht (!) and private tennis courts for those more interested than just swimming. The bedrooms or private bungalows, each in their separate niche, are surrounded by a beautiful garden. The restaurant is also memorable.

HOTEL LA BELLE ETOILE
Hotelier: Marie et Paule Raout-Guillou
Address: 29110 Concarneau, (Finistere)
Tel: (98) 97.05.73
29 Rooms, Expensive
Closed in Oct & Feb
Credit Cards: AX, DC, VS

CONDRIEU   Hotel Beau Rivage   Map# 120

With a terrace setting, Hotel Beau Rivage has some very attractive rooms, a well-known restaurant and lovely views overlooking the Rhone. It is an ideal spot to spend some time relaxing.

HOTEL BEAU RIVAGE
Hotelier: Mme Paule Castaing
Address: 2, Rue du Beau-Rivage
69420 Condrieu, (Rhone)
Tel: (74) 59.52.24 telex: 310917
22 Rooms, Moderate
Open: 13 Feb to 4 Jan
Credit Cards: All Major
U.S. Rep: David Mitchell
Tel: (212) 696-1323 telex: 422123

The medieval village of Conques achieves a dramatic position overlooking the Doudon Canyon.   Tucked a considerable distance off the beaten track, it is a delightful, unspoilt village to explore and is glorious in the gentle light of evening or in the fog of early day.   Conques pride is a classic 13th century church. Directly across from the church, is a simple, but dear hotel, the Ste Foy.   The shuttered windows of our room opened up to the church steeples and we woke to the melodious sound of the bells.   The decor is neat and attractive and one can't fault the location. Dinner is served family style on a sheltered courtyard terrace. The menu offers a number of regional specialties and is very reasonable in price. Portions are plentiful and very good.   The hotel's finest feature is Madame Cannes.   It is her charm, welcoming smile and attitude to please that create the wonderful atmosphere of the Ste Foy.

HOTEL STE FOY
Hotelier: M et Mme Jean Cannes
Address: Conques
12320 St Cyprien
Tel: (65) 69.84.03
20 Rooms, all with private bath
Inexpensive
Open March to October

Once the house of Raymond VII, Comte de Toulouse, Hotel du Grand Ecuyer is a beautiful hotel found at the center of the Vieux Cordes. The rooms are impressive with their large antique beds, many with big fireplaces and magnificent views of the velvet green valley. The hotel has a good restaurant and attractive bar.

HOTEL DU GRAND ECUYER
Hotelier: Yves Thuries
Address: Rue Voltaire
81170 Cordes, (Tarn)
Tel: (63) 56.01.03
15 Rooms, Moderate
Open: April to 15 Oct
Credit Cards: AX, DC

EYNE   Auberge d'Eyne   Map# 66

In the land of narcissis, a millenary farm has been converted into a cozy hotel. It is small and intimate with only eleven rooms and a delightful restaurant. The bar is warmed by an open fire and on warmer days there is a lovely terraced garden to relax in.

AUBERGE D'EYNE
Hotelier: M. Chevallier
Address: 66800 Eyne
Tel: (68) 04.71.12
11 Rooms, Moderate
Open: All Year
Credit Cards: VS, AX, DC

LES EYZIES DE TAYAC   Hotel Cro Magnon   Map# 53

The skull of the famed "old man of Cro Magnon" was unearthed near this town, which is where this vine-covered hotel on the edge of les Eyzies gets its name. The hotel is built on the site of Cro Magnon and its troglodyte.   A beautiful collection of prehistoric flints can be seen in the hotel.   Managed by the third generation of the Leyssales Family this is a tranquil country style hotel. Beautiful perigourdin furnishings are used in the decor.   The hotel is set in a lovely well-shaded garden and has a large, refreshing pool.

HOTEL CRO MAGNON
Hotelier: M et Mme J. Leyssales
Address: 24620 Les Eyzies de Tayac
Tel: (53) 06.97.06
29 Rooms, Moderate
Open: April to 10 October
Credit Cards: All Major
Restaurant

For more than a thousand years this majestic chateau has soaked up the sun and looked upon the beautiful blue water of Cote D'Azur.   The chateau came alive once again as restorations were made to the magnificent Hotel de la Chevre d'Or.   The chateau enjoys a position overlooking the striking coast and dominating the picturesque village of Eze.   Perched high on the mountainside, Eze, with its cobble-stoned streets and craft workshops, is an exciting town to explore.   Then one can literally misplace an entire afternoon on the secluded terrace overlooking the pool with stunning coastline vistas or from the restaurant that crowns it all.   Sprawled along the cobble-stoned streets the bedchambers open onto the riviera or surrounding hillsides.   Often on two levels, the rooms are tastefully appointed with the most modern conveniences. Room number nine deserves special mention.   It is understandably the favorite of the young man who escorted me from room to room.   It hosts its own private terrace and unsurpassed views.   Attentive service, superb cuisine, beautiful views, and a peaceful, serene and medieval atmosphere make the Chateau de la Chevre D'Or, a hotel one will always eagerly return to.

CHATEAU DE LA CHEVRE D'OR
Hotelier: M Bruno-Ingold
Address: Rue de Barri,
06360 Eze Village
Tel: (93) 41.12.12 Telex: 970839
6 Rooms, 3 Apt, Very Expensive
Open: Mid-Feb to Mid-Nov
Credit Cards: AX, VS, DC
U.S. Rep: David Mitchell
Tel: (212) 696-1323 telex: 422123

The Hostellerie du Chateau is a lovely hotel.   There are twenty bedrooms, all individually decorated.   The walls are covered with beautiful materials; the beds are large and comfortable; the bathrooms are often quite spacious; the location peaceful and the views are splendid.   The restaurant has a magnificent menu and the pastries are too tempting to resist!   Room #29 is in the tower, a section of the chateau dating from 1527, with windows on two sides, wedged in amazingly thick walls, overlooking the valley.   Its white laced bedspread and pink and cream colored wall paper make the room feminine and dainty.   Rooms #20 and #12 are both large and lovely apartments.

HOSTELLERIE DU CHATEAU
Hotelier: Blot Family
Address: 02130 Fere en Tardenois
Tel: (23) 82.21.13 telex: 145526
13 Rooms, 7 Apts
Expensive
Open: Mar through Dec
Credit Cards: AX, VS
U.S. Rep: David Mitchell
Tel: (212) 696-1323 telex: 422123

FLEURVILLE Chateau de Fleurville Map# 126

Chateau de Fleurville, a sixteenth and eighteenth century chateau, offers fifteen rooms. Very reasonable in price the accommodations are not deluxe but comfortable and the medieval atmosphere prevails in the public rooms. Wine, dine, and enjoy the quiet and hospitality.

CHATEAU DE FLEURVILLE
Hotelier: M Naudin
Address: 71260 Fleurville
Tel: (85) 33.12.17
15 Rooms, Inexpensive
Open: 15 Dec to 15 Nov
Credit Cards: CB, DC, AX

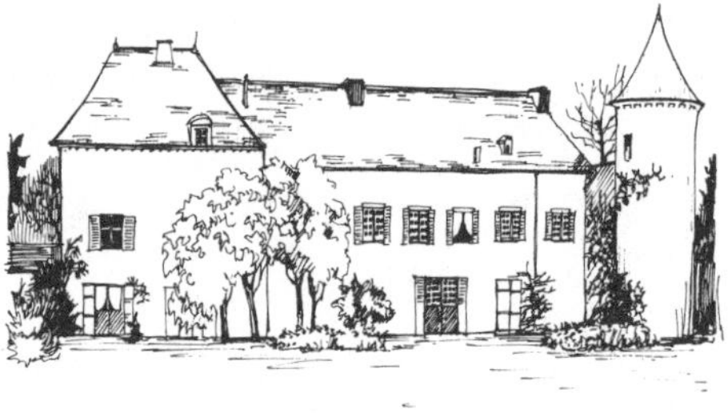

FONTENAY TRESIGNY Manoir de Chaubisson Map# 141

A very deluxe and ornately decorated hotel, Manoir de Chaubisson is surrounded by acres of park and filled with elegance, quality and charm. The restaurant is extremely attractive and its menu has earned a four star rating. Forty miles from Paris, this is a perfect place to relax and forget the traffic, noise and pace of the city.

MANOIR DE CHAUBISSON
Hotelier: M. Sourisseau
Address: RN 4, 77610 Fontenay Tresigny
Tel: (6) 425.91.17 telex: 690635
16 Rooms, Moderate
Open: 15 April to 15 November
Credit Cards: AX, DC, VS
U.S. Rep: David Mitchell
Tel: (212) 696-1323 telex: 422123

FONTVIEILLE EN PROVENCE　　　La Regalido　　　Map # 84

Running the length of this hotel is a beautiful lawn bordered by a multitude of multi-colored flowers. Shade trees abound. I was pleased to find the interior equally attractive and inviting. Converted from an ancient mill, there are a number of pleasant sitting rooms, a tempting restaurant and comfortable bedrooms.

AUBERGE "LA REGALIDO"
Hotelier: Famille Michel
Address: Rue Frederic Mistral
13990 Fontvieille
Tel: (90) 97.70.17
13 Rooms, Expensive
Open: 15 Jan to 30 Nov
Credit Cards: All Major
U.S. Rep: David Mitchell
Tel: (212) 696-1323 telex: 422123

It was a pleasant surprise to discover that this beautiful estate, directly off the road to Arles, is a hotel.   Located outside of town, it is in a quiet location and has a large pool and pleasing rooms.   No restaurant.

LE VAL MAJOUR HOTEL
Address: Route d'Arles
13990 Fontvieille
Tel: (90) 97.70.37
28 Rooms, Inexpensive
Open: 1 Mar to 31 Oct

LA FORET-FOUESNANT   Manoir du Stang   Map# 21

The owner, M Hubert, describes Le Manoir de Fouesnant as "not really a small hotel or inn.   It should be considered as more of a comfortable family home where we receive guests".   It is this attitude, and the sincerity of it, that generates the raves and strong recommendations always associated with this remarkable hotel.   A sixteenth century manor home, it is surrounded by flower gardens, a small lake, woods and acres of farmland.   The interior furnishings manage to retain the original atmosphere of a private estate. The rooms have all the modern conveniences and comforts.   The Louis XV dining room is graceful; the food is always hearty and good.   Rates are on a demi-pension basis.

MANOIR DU STANG
Hotelier: M Guy Hubert
Address: 29133 Foret Fouesnant
(Finistere)
Tel: (98) 56.97.37
26 Rooms
Moderate
Open: 15 May to 20 Sept

GEMENOS   Le Relais de la Magdeleine   Map# 103

This ivy-covered mansion was transformed into a hotel by using taste, care and personal touches.   There is a large refreshing pool.

LE RELAIS DE LA MAGDELEINE
Hotelier: M et Mme Marignane
Address: 13420 Gemenos
Tel: (42) 82.20.05
20 Rooms
Moderate
Open: 15 Mar to 2 Nov

On the outskirts of the medieval perched village of Gordes is the promised seclusion of the hotel "Les Bories". Only four rooms are available in the entire "hotel", you not only feel like, but are the guests in a private home. The restaurant is in a number of rooms. Heavy wooden tables, copper pieces, flowers and a fire all add warmth, while Mme Rousselet supplies the charm and hospitality.

"LES BORIES"
Hotelier: M et Mme Rousselet
Address: 84220 Gordes
Telephone: (90) 72.00.51
4 Rooms
Moderate
Restaurant: Carte 160-235
Open: 1 Jan through Nov

La Mayanelle is run by a personable and friendly Mme Mayard. Located at the heart of the medieval village of Gordes, the rooms of the hotel are not large, (# 4 is the biggest). Ask for a room overlooking the Luberon valley, since the views are magnificent. I was here at the time of a wedding reception and had the only room not occupied by a wedding guest. The atmosphere was happy and gay and influenced my stay considerably.

LA MAYANELLE
Hotelier: M Mayard
Address: 84220 Gordes
Tel: (90) 72.00.28
10 Rooms
Inexpensive
Open: 1 Mar to 1 Jan
Credit Cards: All Major
U.S. Rep: David Mitchell
Tel: (212) 696-1323 telex: 422123

GRAMAT   Chateau de Roumegouse   Map# 76

A small sign directed me along a dirt road and through a small village as I searched for this hotel. I was not certain I had followed the sign correctly. Suddenly, a large majestic tower, peering above the treetops, revealed the location of the Chateau de Roumegouse. A very cordial M Lauwaert, who speaks perfect English, was the only person at the chateau when I arrived. I wrongly assumed that due to the isolated location of the hotel, no one knew about it. As it turned out, the reason for the lack of guests was that M Lauwaert had closed a week early this year. When open the hotel and restaurant are very popular. Even Pompidou and De Gaulle had dined here. The dining rooms are of Louis XV decor. Dinner is served on the terrace overlooking the Lot Valley on summer evenings.

CHATEAU DE ROUMEGOUSE
Hotelier: M Lauwaert
Address: 46500 Gramat, (Lot)
Tel: (65) 33.63.81
11 Rooms, Moderate
Open: 1 April to 30 Nov.
Credit Cards: All Major
U.S. Rep: David Mitchell
Tel: (212) 696-1323 telex: 422123

GUE DES GRUES   Auberge au Gue des Grues   Map # 7

Isolated in the middle of the Dreux forest, along the banks of the Eure, is the small town of Gue des Grues.   (In fact it appeared to me as if the Auberge was the town!).   The hotel only has five bedrooms, which adds to ones sense of peace and isolation.   They are very simple as the focus of this small inn is on its restaurant.   I adored the restaurant.   It is cheery with bright yellow table cloths and scattered flower baskets.   Savoury house specialities are cooked over the large fire which also warms the room.   Personnel are friendly and receptive.

AUBERGE AU GUE DES GRUES
Hotelier: M P. Prevost
Address: Rte de Montreuil
Gue des Grues
28500 Vernouillet
Tel: (37) 43.50.25
5 Rooms, Inexpensive
Open: Feb. through Dec.

The Chateau de Locguenole, surrounded by a forest near the banks of the Blavet River, is dramatic and isolated. Many of the rooms have majestic fireplaces. The views are lovely. Room #9, on the top floor, overpowered by heavy, dark wood beams, is the smallest room but it still manages to be attractive. This chateau has been the family home of the "de la Sabliere" since 1600 and today, rather than sell it, Madame de la Sabliere runs it as an exclusive hotel.

CHATEAU DE LOCGUENOLE
Hotelier: Mme de la Sabliere
Address: 56700 Hennebont
Tel: (97) 76.29.04 telex: 950636
36 Rooms, Expensive
Open: 1 March to 15 November
Credit Cards: AX, DC, EC
U.S. Rep: David Mitchell
Tel: (212) 696-1323 telex: 422123
Pool, Tennis (1985)

Set on the coastal hills just outside the picturesque port town of Honfleur, La Ferme Saint Simeon is a typical Normandy home with flower baskets at each window. Under the management of the Boelen Family, La Ferme Saint Simeon is an excellent hotel. There are ten rooms and nine apartments, and every one is handsomely decorated with fine antiques. The intimate decor of the restaurant is beautifully accented by a beamed ceiling and colorful flower arrangements at each table. The cuisine is delicious, plentiful and expensive (everything is a la carte). Reservations are a must and should be made long in advance.

LA FERME SAINT SIMEON
Hotelier: M et Mme Roland Boelen
Address: Rte A.-Marais, 14600 Honfleur
Tel: (31) 89.23.61 telex: 171031
10 Rooms, 9 Apt, Very Expensive
Closed: Dec. and Jan.
U.S. Rep: David Mitchell
Tel: (212) 696-1323 telex: 422123

HONFLEUR   Hotel du Dauphin   Map# 12

Honfleur is one of the world's most picturesque port towns and I am certain that you will want to linger and absorb Honfleur's character under the enhancements of various lights and moods of the day. On the outskirts of town I have recommended the excellent Ferme Saint Simeon. It is, however, small and expensive. Therefore, should it be full, or, rather your pocketbook not ... there is an alternate ... Hotel du Dauphin. Off the Square Saint Catherine, the hotel's location is both an advantage and disadvantage. Found around the corner is the Vieux Besse or Porte, but at night there is also the buzz of continual traffic and street noise. The rooms are very simple and spartan in their decor but clean and inexpensive. Flower boxes adorn the timbered facade and although the Dauphin does not have a restaurant, it does have an informal bar and cafe.

HOTEL DU DAUPHIN
Hotelier: Philippe Alfandari
Address: 10 pl Pierre Berthelot
14600 Honfleur
Tel: (31) 89.15.53
30 Rooms, Inexpensive
Closed: January
Credit Cards: VS

IGE   Chateau d'Ige

Map # 127

A thirteenth century fortified castle, extremely important in the days of the counts of Macon, is now revived as the marvelous hotel, Chateau d'Ige.   It is located in a small village nestled amongst vineyards.   You will find the rooms very ornate and the specialities truly special.

CHATEAU D'IGE
Hotelier: M Henri Jadot
Address: 71960 Ige, Pierreclos
Tel: (85) 33.33.99 telex: 801194
12 Rooms, Expensive
Open: 15 Mar - 11 Nov
Credit Cards: All Major
U.S. Rep: David Mitchell
Tel: (212) 696-1323 telex: 422123

Hostellerie de Brindos is a superb Spanish chateau, located in the Basque Region. The medieval entry, grand salon and dining rooms are impressive.   Of the many luxurious bedrooms, I particularly liked #17, a corner room facing the lake with its antique four-postered canopy; and #11, a large room, with twin beds, decorated in gold with a round salon.   The hotel is situated on the Lac de Brindos.   It has its own dock, complete with ducks and swans setting a graceful scene.   The chateau is so romantic I found it hard to leave.

CHATEAU DE BRINDOS
Hotelier: M et Mme Vivensang
Address: Lac de Brindos
64600 Anglet, (Pyr. Atl.)
Tel: (59) 23.17.68 telex: 541428
20 rooms, 1 Apt
Expensive
Open: All Year
U.S. Rep: David Mitchell
Tel: (212) 696-1323 telex: 422123
Pool, Tennis

Why would anyone tackle a winding mountain road and travel an hour's distance off the main road paralleling the Rhone Valley to reach the small town of Lamastre? ... A question I posed myself as the sun was setting on what had

already been a full day on the road.   The answer: for the Chateau D'Urbilhac!
Set high above the town, this is a lovely chateau with an expanse of grounds and a
stunning pool.   In keeping with the regal atmosphere staged by the chateau,
the swimming pool is surrounded by statues and enjoys a sweeping panorama of
the valley below.   It was raining at the time of my visit and yet the guests
seemed content to remain indoors.   Very reasonable in price the Chateau seems
to attract European families on holiday.   They appeared very "at home" here
and comfortable even though it was not the summer holiday one would have
anticipated.   Madame Xompero, originally from Brittany, is responsible for a
gracious welcome and is very caring of all her guests.   She is a superb hostess.
Without an elevator, the chateau has rooms scattered on three floors. In what I
am sure were once the servant's quarters, we were in a small but dear room at
the top.   The Chateau d'Urbilhac does also have a number of spacious, grand
rooms: # 14 and # 15 both have beautiful antique double beds, and # 12 a corner
room has antique twin beds and # 24 again twins, but in brass.   The dining room
is small and friendly and the menu boasts a number of regional specialities.
Although the menu terms were unfamiliar to me everything we ordered was
spectacular ... beautifully prepared and thoughtfully served.   Removed many
miles from any major tourist destination,   the Chateau D'Urbilhac offers calm
and quiet, ideal for those who want to relax.

CHATEAU D'URBILHAC
Hotelier: Mme Xompero
Address: Route de Vernoux
07270 Lamastre
Tel: (75) 06.42.11
14 Rooms, Inexpensive
Open: 01 May - 30 Sept
Credit Cards: AX, VS, DC, EC
Gorgeous pool

LEZOUX Chateau de Codignat Map# 42

Chateau de Codignat is a fifteenth century mansion on a ten acre plot. Here you can relish the quiet and seclusion. It has luxurious rooms, a private pool and marvelous meals made from the chateau's own farm products.

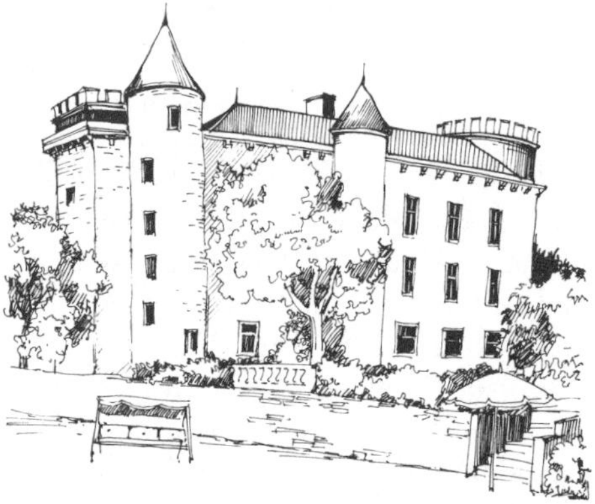

CHATEAU DE CODIGNAT
Hotelier: M et Mme Petit
Address: Bort l'Etang
63190 Lezoux
Tel: (73) 68.43.03
14 Rooms, Expensive
Open: 25 Mar to 30 Nov
Credit Cards: All Major

LIGNY EN CAMBRESIS Le Chateau de Ligny Map# 4

Ligny is a small farming town between Paris and Lille. The location of the seventeenth century Chateau de Ligny promises a quiet vacation. The owner, Mr. Voisin is young and attractive. A small courtyard, in the front, is enclosed by the castle walls and on the other side are pastures fenced off for Mr. Voisin's horses. There are only six bedrooms. Four are with bath and the other two have showers. They are all nice but not spectacular. There is a small bar just off the entry, that is pleasant and the two adjoining rooms serve as the restaurant.

LE CHATEAU DE LIGNY
Hotelier: M Voisin
Address: 59191 Ligny en Cambresis
Tel: (27) 85.25.84 telex: 820211
6 Rooms, Moderate
Closed: January
Credit Cards: VS
U.S. Rep: David Mitchell
Tel:(212) 696-1323 telex: 422123

LISSIEU   Chateau de la Reserve   Map# 121

M and Mme Tournebride, responsible for this fantastic hotel, attempt to conserve a familiar, family atmosphere. The rooms are luxuriously and stylishly decorated; the bathrooms are phenomenal. Words will not do the cuisine justice (but the price certainly does).

CHATEAU DE LA RESERVE
Address: Lissieu
69380 Lozanne, (Rhone)
Tel: (78) 47.60.01
24 Rooms
Very Expensive
Open: 15 Apr to 15 Oct
Restaurant

Domaine de Beauvois is the choice of many who decide to spend some time in the Loire Valley. Recommendations of the guests are always enthusiastic and there are many who return. Domaine de Beauvois is a fifteenth and seventeenth century chateau, surrounded by lovely wooded estate of 350 acres. Its forty rooms are furnished with antiques and offer you a vacation equal to that of the many Lords and Ladys who came to the Loire for relaxation centuries ago. You will find a lovely terrace with a reflecting pool. Fishing, canoeing and sightseeing many chateaux are among the many pleasures open to you. You could find yourself spending weeks here.

DOMAINE DE BEAUVOIS
Hotelier: Patrick C. Ponsard
Address: 37230 Luynes
Tel: (47) 55.50.11 telex: 750204
40 Rooms, Expensive
Open: all year
Credit cards: AX, MC, VS
U.S. Rep: David Mitchell
Tel: (212) 696-1323 telex: 422123

LA MALENE (La Caze)   Chateau de la Caze   Map# 78

After a day of hiking you may return to this fairy tale castle, majestically situated above the Tarn river, and be royally attended to by Mme Roux. Each room is like a king's bedchamber. Room number six is the most beautiful of all.

It has a large wooden canopy and an entire wall of windows overlooking the Tarn and its canyon.   It was the apartment of Sonbeyrane Alamand, a niece of the prior Francois Alamand.   She chose the location and had the chateau constructed in 1489 to serve as her honeymoon haven.   There are paintings on the ceiling of the eight sisters, who later inherited the chateau.   These eight sisters, according to legend, were very beautiful and had secret rendez-vous each night in the garden of the castle with their lovers.

CHATEAU DE LA CAZE
Hotelier: Mme Roux
Address: La Malene
48210 Ste Enimie
Tel: (66) 48.51.01
20 Rooms, Moderate
Open: 1 May to 15 Oct
Credit Cards: AX, VA, DC

LA MALENE   Manoir de Montesquiou   Map# 78

Inhabited by the Barons of Montesquiou for 1500 years, the chateau is located in the small village of La Malene at the center of the Tarn Canyon.   Now a hotel you can enjoy a wonderful meal and then climb the tower to your room.   (The carvings on the headboard in room six are magnificent.)

MANOIR DE MONTESQUIOU
Hotelier: M Bernard Guillenet
Address: La Malene
48210 Ste Enimie
Tel: (66) 48.51.12
12 Rooms, Inexpensive
Open: 4 May to 15 Oct
Credit Cards: DC

MARCAY   Chateau de Marcay   Map # 29

Chateau de Marcay is a typical chateau with two basic end turrets. There are fifteen rooms in the chateau and eleven in a totally modern "motel" annex, where only the essentials are provided. In the chateau, the rooms are each unique and lovely.

CHATEAU DE MARCAY
Hotelier: M Philippe Mollard
Address: Marcay, 37500 Chinon
Tel: (47) 93.03.47 telex: 751475
26 Rooms, Expensive
Open: Mar to January
Credit Cards: AX, VS, DC
U.S. Rep: David Mitchell
Tel: (212) 696-1323 Telex: 422123

Room number eleven is spacious room with twin beds and a dark red color scheme that blends with the richly dark wooden beams. Room number twenty-five is a plain double room, but the bathroom is magnificent and is larger than the room itself and is located in one of the end turrets with blue and white tiles, beamed walls and ceiling. If you spend a lot of your time in the bathroom this room will be a treat. There is also a pool, a garden and a quiet restaurant.

| MARLENHEIM | Hostellerie du Cerf | Map# 138 |

Alsace with its many timbered houses, window boxes colored with geraniums, and sloping vineyards that instill the ever-present excitement of harvest has its own special character and charm. Marlenheim is praised as a typical Alsacian village and the Hostellerie Du Cerf justifiably represents the typical Alsacian Inn. Enjoy an excellent restaurant and the regional specialties and settle in one of the inn's eighteen pleasantly furnished bedrooms.

HOSTELLERIE DU CERF
Hotelier: Robert Husser
Address: 30, Rue du Gal de Gaulle
67520 Marlenheim
Tel: (88) 87.73.73
19 Rooms, Inexpensive
Open: All Year
Credit Cards: AX, DC, CB

Relais la Metairie is a charming country hotel nestled into perhaps the most irresistable region of France, the Dordogne.   It is an attractive stone manor on a plateau of green grass.   La Metairie will assure you of a wonderful and memorable stay.   You will appreciate the tranquility, the cuisine and the inviting fire.

RELAIS LA METAIRIE
Hotelier: Mme Pinget-Vignernon
Address: Millac, 24150 Lalinde
Tel: (53) 22.50.47
10 Rooms, Moderate
Open: 20 Apr to 15 Oct
Credit Cards: AX, EC
U.S. Rep: David Mitchell
Tel: (212) 696-1323 telex: 422123

MAVALEIX   Chateau Hotel de Mavaleix   Map# 51

M and Mme Bercau who took charge of this elegant chateau in 1967, not only offer beautiful bedrooms in the castle but have also cleverly remodeled the barn into a number of pleasingly decorated rooms.   Most of the beautiful bedspreads were hand-made by Mme Bercau's grandmother.   Mme Bercau is gracious and will go to all ends to please her guests.   She once had a museum change its policy and open on a Sunday because it was the only day her guests could go. They have a good restaurant and encourage demi-pension for overnight guests.

CHATEAU HOTEL DE MAVALEIX
Hotelier: M et Mme Bercau
Address: Mavaleix
24800 Thiviers, (Dordogne)
Tel: (53) 52.82.01
30 Rooms, Moderate
Closed: January
Credit Cards: EC, VS

MERCUES	Chateau de Mercues	Map# 74

There is an enchantment about this beautiful castle high above Mercues and the Lot Valley. Once you have seen it you will not be able to take your eyes away or to drive through the valley without stopping. It appears to beckon you. Although it was completely remodeled and renovated in 1968, enabling you to live like a king but with all the modern conveniences, it once served as an ancient noble place which belonged almost twelve centuries to the Lords Bishops of Cahors. It has been restored and decorated in keeping with formal tradition. In the chateau the bedchambers are magnificent. The furnishings are handsome and the windows open up to some splendid valley views. Unique and priced accordingly, room #419 is located in a turret, has windows on all sides and a glassed in ceiling that opens up to the beams of the turret. In recent years there has also been an addition of twenty-three rooms in the newly constructed Pavillon. These bedrooms are modern in decor and less expensive. Built principally to accommodate seminars, some of the rooms have balconies. Before retiring, enjoy a Kir Royal in the castle courtyard and then a memorable dinner in the elegantly beautiful Restaurant L'Aigle D'Or. Through thick medieval walls the landscape of the Lot opens up in full splendor.

The management of the Chateau de Mercues has recently changed. The previous owner passed away unexpectedly and the chateau remained empty for three and a half years. It was then purchased by a local family, the Vigouroux, who are also responsible for some of the regions most sumptuous wines bottled under the Chateau de Haute Serre label. Aware that the owners had changed I returned to Mercues with sentimental remembrances and yet, with a readied attitude to accept any dramatic changes. It was extremely easy to "accept" the new management as, under the direction of the Monsieur Vigouroux, they are attentive and superb. The decor remains unchanged as they bought the chateau intact with all its furnishings. I also had the fortune to meet the owner's daughter, Anne-Catherine. She is a very capable, attractive and bright young woman who is responsible for the marketing of the Chateau de Haut Serre wine. It was also great to learn that the production of Cahor wine has increased in quantity and it is now exported to the United States!

CHATEAU DE MERCUES
Owner: M. Georges Vigouroux
Hotelier: Jean Pierre Leger
Address: Mercues, 46000 Cahors
Tel: (65) 20.00.01 telex: 521307
46 Rooms, Very Expensive
Moderate in Annex
Open: 15 Apr to 31 Oct
Credit Cards: All Major
Pool, tennis, park

In 1952, the chateau which was once the stronghold for the mightiest lords in Provence became a hotel. All of the rooms are beautiful and some are truly exceptional: "Napoleon" with a large canopy and red velvet curtains pulled back into each corner, appears unchanged from the day the lords vacated. The entire hotel is still fit for nobility. The cuisine is "first rate." A small road winds up from the tiny town of Meyrargues to the magnificent chateau. The building is in the shape of a U and shelters a peaceful terrace where you can enjoy a delicious breakfast while enjoying the views.

CHATEAU DE MEYRARGUES
Hotelier: Mme J. C. Drouillet
Address: 13650 Meyrargues
Tel: (42) 57.50.32
14 Rooms, Moderate
Open: 1 Feb to 1 Nov
Credit Cards: AX, DC

MEYREUIS   Chateau D'Ayres   Map# 79

Overpowered by the towering Jonte Canyon Walls, the picturesque buildings of Meyreuis, huddle together along the banks of the Jonte. From this quaint village travel a farm road to the enchanting Chateau d'Ayres. This is a superb hotel hidden behind a high stone wall, that has managed to preserve and protect its special beauty and peace. The chateau was built in the 12th century as a Benedictine monastery. It has been burned, rampaged and even owned by an ancestor claimed by the Rockefellers. It was purchased by the previous owners when the senior Monsieur Teyssier du Cros, a De Nogart, came to ask for the hand of his wife and recognized the grounds where he had played as a child. The Teyssier du Cros family operated the Chateau d'Ayres for a number of years until they sold it in the late 1970s to a young and enthusiastic couple, Jean-Francois and Chantal de Montjou. It is under their care and devotion that the hotel is managed today. Now there are 22 beautiful bedchambers instead of the original two. Works of art are created in the kitchen daily. The Chateau d'Ayres, its character formed by so many events and personalities, is a lovely and attractive hotel.

CHATEAU D'AYRES
Hotelier: M et Mme de Montjou
Address: 48150 Meyreuis
Tel: (66) 45.60.10
23 Rooms, Expensive
Open: 20 Mar to 20 Oct
Credit Cards: DC, VS

Alain Chapel has artfully created an exceptionally lovely place to dine and reside.   Known for his restaurant I was also so very impressed with the decor and intimate charm of the inn.   Fortunate for all, as at the moment there are only thirteen bedrooms, an annex to the hotel is being considered for 1986.

ALAIN CHAPEL
Hotelier: Alain Chapel
Address: 01390 Mionnay
Tel: (7) 891.82.02
13 Rooms, Expensive
Closed: January
Credit Cards: AX, DC

MOELAN SUR MER   Le Moulin du Duc   Map# 22

Alongside a small lake with lily pads, ducks and a few colorful rowboats is the quaint old mill, Hotel le Moulin du Duc.   The dining is exquisite, the owners are charming and the service is wonderful.   The various rooms are in annexes (found alongside the babbling stream).   They are all modern, attractive and offer a comfortable bed where you can sleep well after a filling meal.

LE MOULIN DU DUC
Hotelier: M Quistrebert
Address: 29116 Moelan sur Mer
(Finistere Sud)
Tel: (98) 39.60.73 telex: 940080
22 Rooms, Moderate
Open: 22 Apr to end Oct
Credit Cards: All Major

MONTBAZON   Domaine de la Tortiniere   Map# 31

The only words I can choose to describe the Domaine de la Tortiniere are superlatives.   The chateau has an intricate and fine structure, a lovely pool, and grounds designed for romantic strollers.   The bedrooms are elegant, with a stress on comfort as well.   The dining room is small, attractive and friendly. The cuisine is worth lingering over.   A beautiful woman, Madame Capron excels in charm and as your hostess.   Domaine de la Tortiniere has a casual and inviting atmosphere and provides all the pieces needed to make wonderful lasting memories.

Note: In recent years the chateau has also been sponsoring various cooking classes.   Information available upon request.

DOMAINE DE LA TORTINIERE
Hotelier: M. Capron
Address: 37250 Montbazon
Tel: (47) 26.00.19 telex: 750806
21 Rooms, Expensive
Open: 1 Mar to 15 Nov
Credit cards: MC, EC, VS
Pool

MONTBAZON   Chateau D'Artigny   Map# 31

World famous for its cuisine and accommodations, I feel there is nothing I can write to elaborate.   Chateau D'Artigny, translated into any language, means first class service and a hotel to match.

CHATEAU D'ARTIGNY
Hotelier: Alain Rabier
Address: 37250 Montbazon
Tel: (47) 26.24.24 telex: 750900
48 Rooms, 7 Apt, Very Expensive
Open: 11 Jan to 30 Nov
Credit Cards: All Major
U.S. Rep: David Mitchell
Tel: (212) 696-1323 telex: 422123

The Relais de l'Empereur is situated on a busy main square in the town of Montelimar.   The emperor of this fantastic relais is Napoleon, who stayed in Room #15 on four separate occasions and with four different "amours." Throughout the hotel there are paintings, stain-glassed windows, and artifacts relating to his life.   Mr. Roger Latry, the owner has a wonderful sense of humor, a gift which makes his guests comfortable and relaxed.   The restaurant is excellent.   The rooms are comfortably furnished.

RELAIS DE L'EMPEREUR
Hotelier: M Roger Latry
Address: Place Marx Dormoy
26200 Montelimar
Tel: (75) 01.29.00 telex: 345537
38 Rooms, Moderate
Open: 23 Dec to 10 Nov
Credit Cards: All Major

This is an old manor buffered from the city noise by a surrounding garden.   It has a pleasant restaurant.   The spacious rooms are with bath and are furnished magnificently.   Room #8 has a lovely ornate ceiling and a stunning antique double bed.

HOTEL LE PARC CHABAUD
Address: 16 Ave d'Aygu
26200 Montelimar
Tel: (75) 01.65.66 telex: 345324
22 Rooms, Moderate
Open: 2 Feb to 24 Dec
Credit Cards: AX,DC, VS

| MONTFAVET | Hotel Les Frenes | Map# 87 |

In its own park-like setting, Hotel Les Frenes is a dear inn in a beautifully renovated 19th century burgeoise residence. Les Frenes has sixteen ornately decorated bedrooms. Each is decorated with pieces representative of a certain period. The restaurant is lovely and the menu favors the local cuisine. The town of Montfavet is convenient to Avignon but offers very little in charm or character.

HOTEL LES FRENES
Hotelier: M. J. Biancone
Address: Ave Vertes-Rives
84140 Montfavet
Tel: (90) 31.17.93 telex: 431164
16 Rooms, Expensive
Open: 1 Mar to end Oct
Credit Cards: AX, VS, DC
U.S. Rep: David Mitchell
Tel: (212) 696-1323 telex: 422123

Chateau de Gue Pean offers to the traveler more of an experience than an accommodation. It is not for those seeking luxury and refined service. Rather than describe it myself I would like to duplicate pieces from a marvelous letter written by the Marquis de Keguelin, (the present owner), in order to give you an idea of what to expect. I will just say, because I cannot resist, that the Marquis is a charming and most interesting man, it was an honor to be invited into his private home and share his life style.

..."May I stress our hospitality for paying guests is founded on a simple idea...to extend to the overseas visitor the same hospitality which we offer to our friends, and so enable them to add to the others pleasure of our country a new dimension: that of meeting people in their own homes as their guests and enjoying their company, their cuisine and their culture..."

CHATEAU DE GUE PEAN
Hotelier: Le Marquis de Keguelin
Address: Monthou sur Cher
41400 Montrichard
Tel: (54) 71.43.01 telex: 750382
25 Rooms, Moderate
Open: All Year
Restaurant

Although I did not receive much of a welcome from the swans in the park in front of the chateau (one tried to bite me), the owner and chef, M Lecuyer could not have been nicer.   The beautiful, well preserved Chateau de Saint Jean is hidden behind a park containing 487 different species of trees.   There is a marvelous restaurant in the twelfth century chapelle of the chateau and eight charming and pleasant rooms.   My two favorite rooms were: Room #8 the largest room; room #7, smaller and more feminine.   Wonderful hotel. Just watch out for the swans.

CHATEAU DE SAINT JEAN
Hotelier: M D. Lecuyer
Address: rte Clermont
03100 Montlucon
Tel: (70) 05.04.65
8 Rooms, Moderate
Open: All Year
Credit Cards: AX, VS, DC

On the outskirts of Montpellier, Demeure des Brousses is a marvelous 18th century country house and is removed from the noise and the tension of the city. It thrived for nearly 200 years surrounded by its own vineyards.   It was sadly abandoned until it was purchased and meticulously renovated in 1968.   The Demeure des Brousses is spacious and grand.   The sitting room is inviting.   The eighteen bedrooms are furnished beautifully; all are with bath. Room #16 is the most expensive, and the best, with its own balcony and splendid views. The restaurant, in a neighboring building, is known for its good food. The receptionist spoke wonderful English.

DEMEURE DES BROUSSES
Hotelier: Mme Gasc
Address: Rte de Vauguieres
34000 Montpellier
Tel: (67) 65.77.66
18 Rooms, Moderate
Open: Apr to Oct
Credit Cards: AX, DC

MONTPINCHON   Chateau de la Salle   Map# 16

A more appropriate address for the secluded Chateau de la Salle might read: somewhere in the country. Once a private estate, it is a stone mansion that has only ten bedrooms. The ten rooms available, however, are large, and have either a bath or a shower. They are all handsomely decorated. The small restaurant has a few heavy wooden tables positioned before a warming fire.

CHATEAU DE LA SALLE
Hotelier: Mme Cecile Lemesle
Address: 50210 Montpinchon
Tel: (33) 46.95.19
10 Rooms, Moderate
Open: 25 Mar to 1 Nov
Credit cards: AX, VS, DC
U.S. Rep: David Mitchell
Tel: (212) 696-1323 telex: 422123

MONTREUIL   Relais du Chateau de Montreuil   Map# 5

The twelve rooms are gorgeous and more than made up for the somewhat "cold" reception I received from the woman at the desk.   Room #3 is understandably the room chosen most often by newlyweds.   It has beautiful dark wood walls and floors, large windows overlooking the garden, a soft pink spread on a king-size bed and a beautiful cream-colored oriental rug bordered in pink.   The bathrooms are spacious with lovely tiles and big tubs.

RELAIS DU CHATEAU DE MONTREUIL
Hotelier: C. L. Germain
Address: 4, Chaussee Capucins
62170 Montreuil sur Mer
Tel: (21) 81.53.04
12 Rooms, Moderate
Open: 16 Feb to 30 Nov
U.S. Rep: David Mitchell
Tel: (212) 696-1323 telex: 422123

The home of M and Mme Heyraud is also the Hotel Mere Poulard, enabling you to stretch out your stay on the isolated island of Le Mont St Michel.   The hotel is found immediately on the left as you enter through the town gates.   The rooms, although not extremely large, are comfortable and simply furnished.   The hotel is not elegant but remains as one of the nicest on the island.   It also has a cheery and bright restaurant which is famous for its Poulard omelette.   Although not related to the Heyraud Family there actually was a Mere Poulard who for almost a century ago created an omelette that now the entire village claims fame to. But her omelette is original to the Hotel Mere Poulard and the preparation of it is an attraction in itself.   Cooked in copper pans over an open fire it is hard not to tap one's foot to the sound of the chef as with his whisk he whips the eggs for the next omelette.

Please note: Le Mont St Michel is a popular tourist destination, and in season is mobbed with people.

HOTEL MERE POULARD
Hotelier: M et Mme Bernard Heyraud
Address: 50116 Le Mont St Michel
Tel: (33) 60 14 01
27 Rooms, Moderate
Open: 1 Apr to 30 Sept
Credit Cards: AX, DC

M Peter Holmes and his wife graciously offer the tranquil beauty of their home to people who "seek to escape the noisy fatigue of modern life." The twelfth and thirteenth century chateau lies on the slopes of the Cevennes Mountains, between the towns of Saint Jean du Gard and Lasalle. Its isolated position captures all the calm and beauty of the mountain scenery with the warmth of the Mediterranean Sea. There are seven romantic rooms, wonderfully furnished, and although there is not a restaurant, a buffet is offered in the evening. Chateau de Montvaillant is not a hotel but rather has remained a private home and it would merit a journey just to experience M and Mme Holmes' sincere hospitality.

CHATEAU DE MONTVAILLANT
Hotelier: M et Mme Peter Holmes
Address: Montvaillant
St Croix de Caderle, 30460 Lasalle
Tel: (66) 85.22.71
7 Rooms, Expensive
Open: 27 May to 15 Sept

Whenever I hear the name Le Moulin de Mougins, I will recall the charm and splendor of a small inn, and the promise I made to myself to return to it soon. The hotel, which is actually a sixteenth century mill, is just off the main road from Cannes secluded by its own calm and serene setting. It is only a few miles from the bustling life of the Cote D'Azur, which gives you the best of two worlds. There are only five rooms, each cozy and adorable and a cuisine prepared by the owner himself, Monsieur Roger Verge. During your stay you will receive amazing personal attention. I was followed and helped by so many people, that I kept bumping into them.

LE MOULIN DE MOUGINS
Hotelier: M Roger Verge
Address: Notre Dame de Vie
06250 Mougins
Tel: (93) 75.78.24 telex: 970732
5 Rooms, Very Expensive
Open: 23 Dec-12 Feb & 25 Mar-25 Nov
Credit cards: AX, CB, DC
Cooking School

In 1978 Patrick Gasnier et "sa Brigade" took charge of the Domaine de Rochevilaine and it has dramatically improved under his care and supervision. Rooms that I remembered as spacious but spartan in their furnishings are now handsomely furnished and beautifully appointed. The vast windows of the dining room expose the rocky promontory. There is a distinctive sensation of being shipboard...all you see from the table is the open sea. Beautiful oriental carpets adorn hardwood floors and on sunny days breakfast is enjoyed by many in the well kept gardens that are protected from the open sea breezes by white washed walls.

Domaine de Rochevilaine is dramatically located on Brittany's jagged and rocky coastline. Its setting typifies the most spectacular quality of Brittany. The views from the hotel are stupendous with the sun shining and the sea glistening; or, on a stormy day when the wind howls and the waves crash against the rocks so near your bedroom window.

DOMAINE DE ROCHEVILAINE
Hotelier: M Patrick Gasnier
Address: Pointe de Penlan
Billiers, 56190 Muzillac
(Morbihan)
Tel: (97) 41.69.27 telex: 950570
30 Rooms, Expensive
Open: 15 Apr to 18 Nov
Credit Cards: All Major
U.S. Rep: David Mitchell
Tel: (212) 696-1323 telex: 422123
Pool

Excellent cuisine and cozy accommodations have tempted many to the small and secluded hotel Les Meaulnes.   M Blanchard has turned the cottage into an ideal hideaway.   He has decorated each room with pride, style, taste and has taken time to add those noticeable special touches.   The rooms are named according to decor: Romantique, Empire Rustique, Empire, Louis XV, Louis XIII and Grunier which was once M Blanchard's personal room.   M Blanchard's mother sees that fresh flowers are placed in the rooms daily.   Meals are served to you before the roaring fire in the enchanting restaurant.

LES MEAULNES
Hotelier: M Blanchard
Address: Nancay
18330 Neuvy sur Barangeon
Tel: (48) 51.81.15
8 Rooms
Moderate
Closed: February
Credit Cards: AX, VS, DC

NANS LES PINS   Domaine de Chateauneuf   Map# 101

Thirty miles from Marseille is Domaine de Chateauneuf, an isolated eighteenth century chateau with lovely rooms, appetizing menus and a large pool.   With its history dating back to 1680, the hotel was once a domaine of Monsieur le Comte de Chateauneuf.   It wasn't until 1929 that it was transformed into a hotel.

DOMAINE DE CHATEAUNEUF
Owner: J. Malet
Hotelier: M Gilbert Duval
Address: 83860 Nans les Pins, (Var)
Tel: (94) 78.90.06 telex: 400747
32 Rooms, Expensive
Open: 4 Apr to 1 Nov
Credit Cards: All Major
U.S. Rep: David Mitchell
Tel: (212) 696-1323 telex: 422123

NANTES   Abbaye de Villeneuve   Map# 26

If business or pleasure takes you to Nantes, on the city's outskirts there is a 13th century abbey that has been converted into a hotel.   There is nothing much to say about the village of Les Sorinieres but the Abbaye de Villeneuve creates its own environment.   Set a good distance off, but facing a main road, L'Abbaye is a grand, two story dwelling.   Large ceilings and handsome furnishings impose a formal air and a cordial staff will oversee your needs.   There is a small circular pool on the back lawn, very refreshing on hot summer days.   Two intimate dining rooms as opposed to one large one, provide a small group of guests a lovely, instead of hauntingly vacant, atmosphere. The bedrooms are luxuriously furnished with vast windows and views that open onto the grounds.

ABBAYE DE VILLENEUVE
Hotelier: Philippe Savry
Address: Rte de Sables d'Olonne
44400 Les Sorinieres
Tel: (40) 04.40.25 telex: 710451
16 Rooms, Expensive
Open: All Year
Credit Cards: VS, AX, DC
U.S. Rep: David Mitchell
Tel: (212) 696-1323 telex: 422123
6 miles from Nantes

NIEUIL	Chateau de Nieuil	Map # 45

A long private drive leads you to the hidden beauty and enchantment of the Chateau de Nieuil. It possesses everything a "real" or "fairy tale" chateau should have: dramatic towering turrets, a sleepy moat, intricate gardens and a surrounding forest which was once the favorite hunting spot of kings. All the rooms are handsomely decorated with antiques. My room, an apartment located in one of the turrets, had a magnificent chandelier, paintings, beautiful mirrors, tapestries, attractive wallpaper and an enormous bathroom. The dining room is beautifully paneled and has heavy wood cabinets containing priceless silver pieces. The cuisine is excellent. The owners, M and Mme Pierre Fougerat, have turned the management of the hotel over to their grandson, J. Michel Bodinaud, whose wife, a former art teacher, is the chef. She is also responsible for the creation of an art gallery, housed in the outbuildings facing the castle. The gallery highlights some Aubusson tapestries, old posters, paintings and porcelain.

CHATEAU DE NIEUIL
Hotelier: M JM Bodinaud
Address: 16270 Nieuil
Tel: (45) 71.36.38
13 Rooms, Expensive
Open: 27 Apr to 04 Nov
Credit Cards: AX, VS
U.S. Rep: David Mitchell
Tel: (212) 696-1323 telex: 422123
Pool, Tennis

NIEUL   La Chapelle Saint Martin   Map # 44

La Chapelle Saint Martin rests amid rows of trees.   A velvet green lawn, a small lake in front, and miles of farmland all around complete the storybook atmosphere.   Here you may be served meals in three elegant dining rooms, each is small and private.   The accommodations are inviting.   La Chapelle Saint Martin is only a few minutes from Limoges, a city famous for its porcelain.

LA CHAPELLE SAINT MARTIN
Hotelier: M Jacques Dudognon
Address: St Martin du Faulx
87510 Nieul
Tel: (55) 75.80.17
10 Rooms,1 Apt, Moderate
Open: Mar to Jan
Tennis

Nimes is a fun, lively city and the Hotel Imperator gives you the chance to stay here a while longer.   Located across from the park it manages to find some peace and quiet in the middle of Nimes.   All the rooms are with either shower or bath.   Each is spacious and decorated with antiques and those facing the garden are only eleven francs more.   Some rooms have balconies at no extra cost, so you definitely should make a point of asking for one.

HOTEL IMPERATOR
Address: Place Aristide Briand
30000 Nimes
Tel: (66) 21.90.30 telex: 490635
61 Rooms, Moderate
Open: 15 Mar to 15 Jan
Credit Cards: All Major
U.S. Rep: Best Western
Tel: (800) 334-7234

NOVES   Auberge de Noves   Map# 88

L'Auberge de Noves is just a few minutes south of Avignon.   The original construction dates from 1810 but was completely renovated and modernized in 1955. The Lalleman family have much to offer you.   Here you will find quality cuisine, comfortable rooms, a heated pool, good service and a tranquil ambiance.

As the Lalleman's explain, "We consider ourselves as a restaurant with rooms and not as a hotel with restaurant." Therefore rooms are rented on a demi-pension basis only.

AUBERGE DE NOVES
Hotelier: Lalleman Family
Address: 13550 Noves
Tel: (90) 94.19.21 telex: 431312
22 Rooms, Expensive
Open: 3 Feb to 3 Jan
Credit Cards: AX, VS
U.S. Rep: David Mitchell
Tel: (212) 696-1323 telex: 422123

ONZAIN   Domaine des Hauts de Loire   Map# 33

Domaine des Hauts de Loire is a beautiful chateau opened this past decade as a hotel. It is managed and owned by Mme Bonnigal, who also oversees the successful Hostellerie de Chateau at Chaumont sur Loire. It was purchased by her when the original owner died and left to his children, who in turn decided to sell and divide up the inheritance. It had just turned dark as I neared the chateau a mile or so from the town of Onzain. I drove slowly and cautiously up the long road because of the many rabbits and in order to get a glimpse of the gorgeous chateau, silver in the moonlight, revealed fleetingly through the trees. The chateau has twenty-six rooms, all large and elegantly decorated. The bathrooms are spacious and modern. The dining room is quite lovely.

DOMAINE DE HAUTS DE LOIRE
Hotelier: Mr P.A. Bonnigal
Address: 41150 Onzain
Tel: (54) 20.72.57 telex: 751547
26 Rooms
Expensive
Open: 15 Mar to 15 Nov
Credit Cards: All Major

PAU   Hostellerie du Canastel   Map # 62

Hostellerie de Canastel is a good place to stop to break your journey. It is a simple roadside inn convenient to the Basque region as well as the pilgrimage city of Lourdes. Ideal for the hot summer months, it has a lovely pool bordered by a patio and enclosed by greenery. There are twelve pleasing rooms and all have beautiful bathrooms. Four of the rooms are in an annex and open directly onto the pool area. In the main building, the rose room (double) and the blue room (twin), overlook the pool rather than the road. The restaurant is good.

HOSTELLERIE DU CANASTEL
Hotelier: Mme Bensoussan
Address: Ave Rausky
Route Oloron, 64110 Jurancon
Tel: (59) 06.13.40
12 Rooms, Inexpensive
Open: all year, Pool

In one of Perouges' old, timbered buildings that no longer stands erect but rather, leans out over the narrow, cobble-stoned streets, you will find a darling restaurant of the Ostellerie du Vieux Perouges.   Enhancing the atmosphere are waiters dressed in regional costumes.   In two separate buildings, also located in the charming medieval town of Perouges, are some majestic rooms of the Ostellerie.   The fifteen rooms of the Manoir are fabulously decorated with antiques and a few even enjoy the calm of their own garden.   Ten rooms, much simpler in decor are located in another building.

OSTELLERIE DU VIEUX PEROUGES
Hotelier: M. Georges Thibaut
Address: Place du Tilleul
Vieux Perouges
01800 Meximieux
Tel: (74) 61.00.88
25 Rooms, Expensive
Open: All Year
Credit Cards: VS

There are certain characteristics and qualities I will always recall and associate with each of the hotels I have visited.   My stay at the Chateau de Violet will forever draw memories of an encouraging, friendly welcome and the amazing woman responsible for it, Mme Faussie.   She and her husband purchased the chateau twenty years ago.   Mme Faussie is in charge of the hotel and M Faussie takes care of the vineyards.   There are fifteen rooms, two of which are very nice; Empire and Archeveque.   The others are nice but simple in decor.   The restaurant is good and the service is exceptionally gracious.

CHATEAU DE VIOLET
Hotelier: M et Mme Faussie
Address: 11160 Peyriac Minervois
Tel: (68) 78.10.42
15 Rooms, Moderate
Open: all year
Credit Cards: All Major
Pool

PLEVEN   Manoir de Vaumadeuc   Map# 18

Manoir de Vaumadeuc is gorgeous.   Located twelve miles from Brittany's coast in the Hunaudaye Forest, this fifteenth century manor has a peaceful environment and has retained its medieval flavor.   Le Manoir is an excellent hotel managed by Mme de Pontbriand.   She and her personnel create a genial home-like feeling.   There are ten handsome bedchambers.   Furniture, elegant tapestries, paintings, beamed ceilings, views and small items in each room, (a chest filled with antique odds and ends, a case of colorful lead soldiers) catch your attention and hint at the special qualities and personal touches which make Le Manoir de Vaumadeuc unique.

MANOIR DE VAUMADEUC
Hotelier: Mme de Pontbriand
Address: Pleven
22130 Plancoet
Tel: (96) 84.46.17
10 Rooms, Expensive
Open: 15 Mar to 03 Jan
Restaurant

POLIGNY   Hostellerie des Monts de Vaux   Map# 130

The Hostellerie des Monts de Vaux, on the road from Switzerland, has charm and character.   It is the Carrion family home and they enjoy having you as their guests.   They request that you reserve rooms on a demi-pension basis.

HOSTELLERIE DES MONTS DE VAUX
Hotelier: Carrion Family
Address: 39800 Poligny
Tel: (84) 37.12.50
10 Rooms, Expensive
Open: 01 Jan to 30 Oct
U.S. Rep: David Mitchell
tel: (212) 696-1323 telex: 422123

M and Mme Foltz are perhaps two of the warmest people ever to open a hotel. Auberge du Vieux Puits is a typical Normandy home, with the original timbers, which date from the 17th century. It was used as a tannery in the 19th century and converted into an inn in 1921. It has been in the Foltz family for three generations. A large portion was tragically destroyed by bombs during the war. The present M and Mme Foltz were only able to salvage and remodel eight of the original twenty rooms. The eight rooms are small, modest yet extremely charming. Five of the rooms are equipped with showers. It is a real treat to be awakened in the morning by a cheerful girl and a tray of hot coffee and a delicious assortment of hot rolls. The Auberge du Vieux Puits may only have eight rooms but it also has four individual and cozy restaurants. It is known for its cuisine and M Foltz is always making improvements on what one orders, he never seems to feel that they have made the best choice from the specialities he has to offer.

AUBERGE DU VIEUX PUITS
Hotelier: M et Mme Foltz
Address: 6 rue Notre-Dame du Pre
27500 Pont Audemer
Tel: (32) 41.01.48
8 Rooms, Inexpensive
Open: 20 Jan to 02 July
   and: 11 July to 20 Dec
Credit Cards: VS

Tucked away in the beauty and quiet of the Black Mountains is a fantastic hotel definitely worth searching for. Once you've arrived at the Chateau de Montledier and developed a taste for the splendor and elegance it offers you will never want to leave but when you do you'll never forget the route back. The rooms are magnificent. Raymond, in my opinion is the loveliest of all. It has two stunning antique canopies and a spacious, modern bathroom. The restaurant in the cellar is quite cozy and intimate. The cuisine is marvelous and the service impressive. Everything is done to perfection and with superb taste.

CHATEAU DE MONTLEDIER
Hotelier: M Francis Sidobre
Address: Route d'Angles
Pont de l'Arn, 81200 Mazamet
Tel: (63) 61.20.54
10 Rooms, Expensive
Closed: January
U.S. Rep: David Mitchell
Tel: (212) 696-1323 telex: 422123

Tradition and elegance are forever associated with Moulin de Vernegues.   Lord Damian's beautiful dwelling place has been restored, leaving the romantic, rustic air untouched and adding all the modern needs.   The rooms overlook the peaceful fields and the restaurant is superb.   Sporting possibilities are hunting, horse-back riding, tennis, fishing, strolling...

MOULIN DE VERNEGUES
Hotelier: M Ventre
Address: Pont Royal 13370 Mallemort
Tel: (90) 59.12.00 telex: 401645
37 Rooms, Moderate
Open: all year
Credit cards: All Major
U.S. Rep: David Mitchell
Tel: (212) 696-1323 telex: 422123
Pool, tennis

Le Clos Saint Vincent is not only on the wine route but also right in the middle of a vineyard.   A sign directs you up a small road which winds through the vineyard to the hotel.   Positioned high on the hill, it has marvelous views of the Alsacian Valley all the way to the Black Forest in Germany.   The rooms are individually identified by a different flower or fruit pattern.   They are all with bath.   The restaurant is very well known for its wine and menu.

LE CLOS SAINT VINCENT
Hotelier: M Chapotin
Address: Rte de Bergheim
68150 Ribeauville
Tel: (89) 73.67.65
11 Rooms, Expensive
Open: March to November
U.S. Rep: David Mitchell
Tel: (212) 696-1323 telex: 422123

RIEC SUR BELON   "Chez Melanie"   Map# 23

If you are anywhere near the vicinity of Brittany you must make a stop at the Restaurant-Hotel "Chez Melanie." It is a simple, white, three storey building, with three rows of shuttered windows, and colorful flower boxes, located on a side street in the small town of Riec sur Belon. There are a number of quaint dining rooms where you can feast on famous specialities colorfully served to you by girls in traditional costume. I arrived on a Saturday afternoon and a wedding reception occupied the entire place. Children were gaily running about from room to room and through the garden; the older gentlemen had gathered in the bar to smoke and drink and the women, also in costume, were still chatting over coffee. Although she definitely had a million people to attend to, M Trellu, the owner, welcomed me with open arms, and if I wasn't personally there amongst all the commotion, I would have believed she had all the time in the world. She is literally charm personified. "Chez Melanie" is famous for its restaurant, but there are a few rooms available if you can't bare to leave the friendly and gay atmosphere. They are small, but pleasant and immaculate. A few have baths.

"CHEZ MELANIE"
Hotelier: Mme G. Trellu
Address: Place de l'Eglise
29124 Riec sur Belon
Tel: (98) 06.91.05
7 Rooms, Inexpensive
Open: All Year
Credit Cards: AX, DC

RIGNY   Chateau de Rigny   Map# 133

The Chateau de Rigny deserves notice.   The mannequin on a ledge well above
the fireplace was the first thing to catch my eye!   This is the only "unusual"
item, afterwards there is the beauty of the garden; the calmness of the Soane
River; the excellence of the cuisine and the grandeur of the rooms to draw your
attention.

CHATEAU DE RIGNY
Hotelier: Mme de Billy
Address: Rigny, 70100 Gray
Tel: (84) 65.25.01
23 Rooms, Moderate
Open: All Year
Credit Cards: All Major
Tennis

On top of a hill, dominating a town only a few miles from Orange, yet seemingly far removed from civilization, you find a dramatic chateau which has now been converted into a hotel.   A twelfth century dungeon, vaulted chambers, swords, elegant bed chambers, all make it easy for you to forget that you are in a hotel and let you wander into the past from the very instant you enter the courtyard.

CHATEAU DE ROCHEGUDE
Hotelier: Mon. Chabert
Address: 26130 Rochegude
Tel: (75) 04.81.88 telex: 345661
29 Rooms, Expensive
Open: 1 Mar to 1 Nov
Credit Cards: All Major
Restaurant, Pool, Tennis

LA ROCHE L'ABEILLE   Moulin de la Gorce   Map# 43

Set amongst rolling hills of farmland is a 16th century mill converted into a hotel and a fantastic restaurant.   In the various buildings clustered along the edge of a quiet pond and stream are some luxuriously furnished bedrooms, filled with antiques and whose walls are hung with tapestries. (The tapestries are hand painted replicas from a factory in Rambouillet, and are for sale.)   The atmosphere of the restaurant is surpassed only by the unusually beautiful presentation of each course.   The care and attention to detail that the

Bertranet family strive for is evident throughout. There are currently only six rooms in the mill but the Bertranets have plans to build an additional three in the next year. A lovely retreat.

MOULIN DE LA GORCE
Hotelier: M et Mme Bertranet
Address: La Roche L'Abeille
87800 Nexon
Tel: (55) 00.70.66
9 Rooms, Moderate
Closed: January
Credit Cards: All Major

ROUFFACH   Chateau D'Isenbourg   Map# 134

With the opening of this fabulous hotel only ten years ago, a trip to Alsace can now be even more memorable and enjoyable. During the middle ages the Chateau d'Isenbourg was the cherished home of the "prince bishops" of Strasbourg and more recently it was owned by wealthy wine growers. On the hillside above the town of Rouffach, the chateau is still surrounded by its own vineyards. You can appropriately savor your delicious meal and fine Alsacian wines in the vaulted wine cellars which now serve as a very pleasant restaurant. There are forty rooms, nine of which are new additions. A number of rooms are exceptionally elegant due to the impressive, hand-painted ceilings. Room number 1, a beautiful apartment, and number 2, not an apartment but even so, quite spacious, were two such rooms. Room 14, is not as expensive as an apartment but is practically the same size and also quite lovely. All the rooms are with bath. There is also a large pool.

CHATEAU D'ISENBOURG
Hotelier: M Daniel Dalibert
Address: 68250 Rouffach
Tel: (89) 49.63.53
40 Rooms, Expensive
Open: 15 Mar to 15 Jan
Credit Cards: VS
U.S. Rep: David Mitchell
Tel: (212) 696-1323 telex: 422123

SAINT GERMAIN EN LAYE   Cazaudehore   Map# 2

Just a few miles from Paris and the exciting and busy life it offers, is a charming inn in the heart of the forest of St. Germain en Laye. The pace is relaxed, the surroundings are beautiful and green and the accommodations and restaurant of the hotel La Forestiere are marvelous.

CAZAUDEHORE ET LA FORESTIERE
Hotelier: M et Mme Cazaudehore
Address: 1 ave du President Kennedy
78100 St Germain en Laye
Tel: (3) 973.36.60 telex: 696055
30 Rooms, Expensive
Open: All Year
Credit Cards: VS
U.S. Rep: David Mitchell
Tel: (212) 696-1323 telex: 422123

On the water's edge, "au port", the activity and scenes of this Mediterranean village are framed by the windows of La Voile D'Or.   The marina with its many yachts and fishing boats is simply part of the hotel's decor.   Soft provencal pastels and countryside furnishings create a relaxed atmosphere.   The restaurant affords sophisticated dining and the refined attentive service make the Voile D'Or a favorite of some of the most discriminating clientele.

LA VOILE D'OR
Hotelier: J.R. Lorenzi
Address: 06230 St Jean Cap Ferrat
Tel: (93) 01.13.13 telex: 470317
50 Rooms, Very Expensive
Open: 25 Feb to 30 Oct
2 Pools, Beach, Tennis

SAINT JEAN DE LUZ   Hotel de Chantaco   Map# 65

HOTEL DE CHANTACO
Owner: M P. Larramendy
Hotelier: Libouban-Priffer
Address: 64500 St Jean de Luz
Tel: (59) 26.14.76
24 Rooms, Expensive
Open: Easter to October
Credit Cards: AX, DC

Hotel Chantaco is a lovely Spanish Villa opposite a beautiful golf course, in an isolated and quiet position on the outskirts of St Jean de Luz. Facing an excellent 18 hole golf course, it serves as an ideal retreat. The decor is a bit spartan but fitting for the weathered villa. The rooms, service and restaurant are wonderful and add to the enchantment of the Basque Province.

SAINT LATTIER   Le Lievre Amoureux   Map# 118

Le Lievre Amoureux is the result of the dreams of an extremely warm family who wanted to open a hotel where people could feel as relaxed as they are at home, but even more comfortable. The cuisine, prepared by M Caillat, is delicious and Mme and Mlle Caillat have beautifully decorated all the rooms. The family now welcomes and graciously attends to their guests. In addition to seven rooms in the Pavillon, (adjacent to the restaurant), there is a little cottage on the hill with four lovely bedrooms, a private dining room and a modern, equipped kitchen. It serves as an ideal hideaway for couples or a group of friends. My opinion is that their dream has come true. You'll find Le Lievre Amoureux is better than home and you'll never care to leave.

LE LIEVRE AMOUREUX
Hotelier: Caillat Family
Address: 38840 Saint Lattier
Tel: (76) 36.50.67
7 Rooms, Moderate
Open: 15 Mar to 15 Nov
Credit Cards: AE, DC

On the left hand side of the road as you approach the old town, a warm smile and an excellent hotel welcome you to Saint Paul.   From the Hotel Les Orangers nestled amongst olive and orange trees, you have a wonderful view of Saint Paul and the French Riviera.   The hotel is no longer associated with the neighboring restaurant, Les Oliviers.   The ten rooms are in a building off the reception and are joined by a large living room with a cozy fireplace.   Mme Biancheri's supervision is apparent throughout.   Each room is exceptionally well done, with a lovely large bathroom, balcony and its own individual charm.   She has skillfully decorated the bedrooms.   The curtains were all freshly pressed and I adored having our own terrace.   Not yet ripe, grapes clung to the vines in the terrace corner and orange trees blossomed just below and seemingly all of Provence spread before us.

LES ORANGERS
Hotelier: Mme Biancheri
Address: 06570 St Paul de Venc
Tel: (93) 32.80.95
10 Rooms, Expensive
Open: All Year

Another beautiful hotel, positioned in the old quarter of Saint Paul de Vence. There are many attractive salons, a beautiful restaurant where you will discover the cuisine both excellent and expensive, refreshing pool and rustic rooms. Le Colombe D'Or boasts a fantastic collection of art. In the past a number of famous painters paid for their meals with their talents ... and the reputation of the inn dictates that one merits the other!

HOTEL LE COLOMBE D'OR
Hotelier: M et Mme Roux
Address: Place de Gaulle
06570 St Paul de Vence
Tel: (93) 32.80.02 telex: 970607
24 Rooms, Very Expensive
Open: 15 Dec to 03 Nov
Credit Cards: All Major

SAINT PAUL DE VENCE   Le Hameau   Map # 113

Renovated from an old farm complex the bedrooms of this inn are found in four buildings clustered together on grounds dressed with fruit trees and flowers. Each building has its own character and name: L'Oranger, L'Olivier, Le Pigeonnier and La Treille. Three of the largest rooms have a small room for an infant and the attraction of their own private balconies, (#1 and #3 with twin beds and #2 with a double bed). Of the rooms I saw our room was actually my favorite. Room #11 has two striking antique twin beds, a lovely view onto the garden, spacious bathroom and an adjoining sitting room. I was very impressed with the quality of this provencal inn. Monsieur Xavier Huvelin is a charming host and is graciously attentive to the needs of his guests. Le Hameau does not have a restaurant but a delicious country breakfast can be enjoyed in the garden or in the privacy of your room. An excellent hotel for an extremely reasonable price.

LE HAMEAU
Hotelier: M et Mme X. Huvelin
Address: 528 Rte de la Colle
06570 St Paul de Vence
Tel: (93) 32.80.24
16 Rooms, Moderate, Credit Cards: AX
Open: 1 Feb to 1 Nov
U.S. Rep: Jacques de Lorsay
Tel: (800) 223-1510

SAINT PONS   Chateau de Ponderach   Map # 69

Chateau de Ponderach is a wonderful stopping place. Surrounded by many acres of greenery in a region with a mild Mediterranean climate, the chateau has eleven rooms, all of which are individual in style and pleasant. A good restaurant.

CHATEAU DE PONDERACH
Hotelier: Mme P. Counotte
Address: 34220 St Pons
Tel: (67) 97.02.57
11 Rooms, Moderate
Open: 1 Apr to 15 Oct
Credit Cards: All Major
U.S. Rep: David Mitchell
Tel: (212) 696-1323 telex: 422123

Located on the top of a hill, in the heart of the province of Vivarais and looking down upon fifty acres of park, the Chateau de Besset, an authentic 15th century chateau converted into a first-class hotel, offers comfort and quiet to its visitors.   The rooms, each characteristic of a certain style, are elegant and grand with spacious bathrooms.   The restaurant has choice food and local wines to be served in the company of a large burning fire.   Very expensive.

CHATEAU DE BESSET
Owner: M Roger Gozlan
Hotelier: Guy Thenard
Address: St. Romain de Lerps
07130 St Peray
Tel: (75) 44.41.63
6 Rooms 4 Apt, Very Expensive
Open: 16 Apr to 14 Oct
Credit Cards: AX, VS, DC
U.S. Rep: David Mitchell
Tel: (212) 696-1323 telex: 422123
Pool

SALLES CURAN   Hostellerie du Levezou   Map# 73

The true French meaning behind their saying, "Chez Soi," can be defined and experienced at the Hostellerie du Levezou.   It is run by the entire M Bouviala family: parents, sons, daughters and the dog. Inside this fourteenth century chateau you will find rooms that are simple, yet comfortable and cheery and an attractive restaurant with a large fireplace where M Bouviala grills many of his delicious specialties. It is the sort of place you long to return to, and apparently everyone does.

HOSTELLERIE DU LEVEZOU
Hotelier: M Bouviala
Address: 12410 Salles Curan
Tel: (65) 46.34.16
30 Rooms, Inexpensive
Open: 1 Apr to 15 Oct
Credit Cards: All Major
Dates Open: 15 Mar to 1 Nov

SALON DE PROVENCE   Abbaye de Sainte Croix   Map# 89

An atmospheric abbey, built in the ninth and twelfth centuries, is now the Abbaye De Sainte-Croix, a luxurious twenty-two room relais. Sprawling along the contours of the hillsides above Provence the abbey secures a peaceful and idyllic location for a hotel and enjoys a splendid panorama of Provence. Under vaulted ceilings antiques, tiled floors and open fires warm the atmosphere of the Abbaye. The restaurant highlights provencale specialties.

ABBAYE DE SAINTE CROIX
Hotelier: M et Mme Yves Bossard
Address: Route du Val-de-Cuech
13300 Salon de Provence
Tel: (90) 56.24.55 telex: 401247
22 Rooms, Very Expensive
Open: 1 Mar to 31 Oct
Credit Cards: All Major
U.S. Rep: David Mitchell
Tel: (212) 696-1323 telex: 422123
Large private pool

SARE   Hotel Arraya   Map# 63

Nestled in the region bordering Spain, the Arraya has captured the tradition and rustic flavor of Basque.   Nine miles from the coastal town of St. Jean de Luz, the inn is decorated with an abundance of antiques.   A former wayside inn on the pilgrimage road to Santiago de Compostela, the Hotel Arraya is decorated in the style of the finest Basque residences of the 17th century.   The entry, lobby and breakfast nook are dressed with charm.   Cozy blue and white gingham cushions pad the wooden chairs that are set round a lovely collection of antique tables.   The restaurant offers regional basque specialties and one must stay here long enough to sample them all.   Pate de Foie Gras, cepes, salamis (special sauce), country hams, goat cheese made by the mountain shepherds and Pastiza, a delicious basque, almond cake filled with either cream or black cherry preserves.   The hotel is managed by Paul Fagoaga and he is present to welcome his guests as friends, or "zizilua" in the native dialect.

HOTEL ARRAYA
Hotelier: M. Paul Fagoaga
Address: Sare, 64310 Ascain
Tel: (59) 54.20.46
20 Rooms, Inexpensive
Open: 15 May to 31 Oct
Credit Cards: AX, CB

| SCIEZ BONNATRAIT | Chateau de Coudree | Map# 132 |

On the French side of the Lac Lemain is a majestic 13th century chateau that has preserved its medieval atmosphere and added an air of elegance. The rooms are enchanting, the cuisine is marvelous and the pool will be welcome on the hot days.

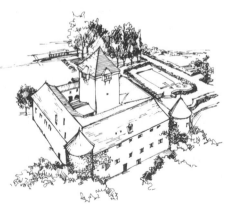

CHATEAU DE COUDREE
Hotelier: Famille Laden
Address: Sciez Bonnatrait
74140 Douvaine
Tel: (50) 72.62.33 telex: 385417
20 Rooms, 2 Apt, Expensive
Open: April to October
U.S. Rep: David Mitchell
Tel: (212) 696-1323 telex: 422123

Sometimes it takes staying at a place to understand and realize its charms. The Domaine de Bassibe is set off a country   road in a region popular for its health spas and resorts.   It is a beautiful vine covered homestead in a tranquil setting. The decor, however, quite modern does not blend well with the character of the building and had I just seen, rather than stayed at the Bassibe, I doubt that it would now be included in the book.   But, given a day to linger by the poolside with cornfields at one's side and farmland stretching out in the distance; to watch a couple request lunch on the pool lawn and then receive a table complete with linens, crystal and then an elegant presentation of a meal and the quality of service one would expect in the finest of restaurants; and to experience the warm hospitality of the staff ... I've decided I want to return here and want to share the inn with you.   The Bassibe seemed to provide a romantic hideaway for the couple on the lawn as well as an ideal vacation spot for a number of families. The restaurant, set in the shade under the trees at lunch and in the converted stables at dinner, proved popular with the guests of the hotels and locals as well. I longed for a break between journeys in Basque before continuing on to the Dordogne and the Domaine de Bassibe served as the perfect, tranquil retreat!

DOMAINE DE BASSIBE
Hotelier: Jean Pierre Capelle
Address: Segos, 32400 Riscle
Tel: (62) 09.46.71 telex: 531918
9 Rooms, Expensive
Open: 15 Apr to 15 Oct
Credit Cards: AX, VS, DC
U.S. Rep: David Mitchell
Tel: (212) 696-1323 telex: 422123

Grand in the tradition and service that was once fitting of the British Parliamentary Clerks to the Council of Europe, the Hotel Gutenberg is a genuine sample of Alsacian atmosphere and comfort.   Today Mme Lette extends a warm welcome to her 1745 mansion, conveniently located near the Place Gutenberg.

HOTEL GUTENBERG
Hotelier: M et Mme Pierre Lette
Address: 31 Rue Serruriers
67000 Strasbourg
Tel: (88) 32.17.15
50 Rooms, Inexpensive
Open: All Year
No Restaurant

TALLOIRES   Auberge de Pere Bise   Map# 131

A traditional welcome, a refined table, one of the best in the region; a beautiful location and hotel will assure success to your vacation.   Auberge du Pere Bise, a shingled, three-story, ivy-covered inn is charming through and through.   Here you can enjoy the lake, mountains and a large, wooded park.

AUBERGE DE PERE BISE
Hotelier: Charlyne Bise
Address: Rte de Port, Talloires
74290 Veyrier du Lac
Tel: (50) 60.72.01 telex: 385812
34 Rooms, Very Expensive
Open: 18 Jan-16 Apr & 4 May-20 Dec
Credit Cards: AX, VS, DC
U.S. Rep: David Mitchell
Tel: (212) 696-1323 telex: 422123

TALLOIRES   L'Abbaye   Map# 131

Hotel L'Abbaye is an impressive complex of stone buildings on the banks of the Lake Annecy.   In the summer and springtime you can either dine or leisurely sit on an open terrace bordered by fresh and colorful flowers.   The old Abbaye has thirty-three rooms, all lovely; a marvelous restaurant with its numerous specialties; a relaxing sauna but no pool.

L'ABBAYE
Hotelier: Claude Tiffenat
Address: Talloires
74290 Veyrier du Lac
Telephone: (50) 67.40.88
33 Rooms, Expensive
Open: 1 May to 15 Oct
Credit Cards: All Major
U.S. Rep: David Mitchell
Tel: (212) 696-1323 telex: 422123

On the other side of the peninsula from Cannes, high above the coastal road is an isolated hillside, villa-hotel.   Views of the sea, either from the casual terrace restaurant, or from the slightly more elegant, glassed-in dining room are fabulous.   The waitresses are very courteous and polite.   There are a dozen overnight rooms for guests wishing to linger in this quiet, isolated spot, with its startling views and prospects of an untroubled night.

VILLA ANNE GUERGUY
Hotelier: Guerguy Family
Address: La Galere,
06590 Theoule, (Alpes-Mar.)
Telephone: (93) 75.44.54
14 Rooms, Expensive
Open: 1 Feb to 31 Oct
Restaurant: La Galere

TOURTOUR   Bastide de Tourtour   Map# 104

Located on the outskirts of the town, the Bastide is actually above Tourtour, "the city in the heavens."   All of the provencial-styled rooms have a bath and twelve have private terraces.   Being on the top of the world, or at least of Provence, you have splendid views of the region.   The old provencal village of

Tourtour is just 500 meters from the hotel. There is a beautiful pool with an outdoor grill (Summer use only), delicious food and a very pleasant and friendly atmosphere.

BASTIDE DE TOURTOUR
Hotelier: M et Mme Laurent
Address: Route Draguignan
Tourtour, 83690 Salernes
Tel: (94) 70.57.30 telex: 970827
26 Rooms, Expensive
Open: 15 Jan to 15 Dec
Credit Cards: AX, VS, DC
U.S. Rep: David Mitchell
Tel: (212) 696-1323 telex: 422123
Pool, Tennis, Ping Pong

| TREBEURDEN | Ti Al-Lannec | Map# 19 |

From a hilltop position overlooking neighboring islands is a delightful hotel managed and run by an equally delightful couple. Gerard et Danielle Jouanny purchased what in 1977 was a private home then put their own energies and creative effort into renovating and opening it as a hotel in 1978. The Ti Al-Lannec still achieves the feeling of a home away from home, from the smell of croissants baking to the personal touches in the decor. The restaurant is lovely and opens onto glorious views of the coast. The public rooms have been thoughtfully equipped to accommodate the hobbies of the guest and the unpredictable moods of the weather. There were jigzaw puzzles, books, games, in addition to a swingset on the lawn and an outdoor, knee-high chess set. From the back lawn there is also a private path that descends to the beach. The presence of children is obvious as is their welcome. The hotel was full, but as I viewed a number of occupied rooms, there were few that did not have a cherished stuffed animal warming the pillow! Mme Jouanny's feminine touch is seen by the choice of sweet prints that decorate a majority of the rooms. They are truly individual, but all extremely comfortable for extended stays and have bright modern bathrooms. Most of the rooms look out to the sea and this winter plans are to add balconies and terraces to most all of the rooms. I saw an especially lovely corner room, number 11, spacious, twin beds and fantastic views.

When I explore hotels I make my own mental list of places I want to make a special effort to return to when I am on vacation. I was very impressed by the Ti Al-Lannec but I am not at all certain that it wasn't Danielle Jouanny's sweet, warming smile that didn't touch me even more. She has a lovely, gentle air of sophistication and makes a perfect host.

TI AL-LANNEC
Hotelier: Gerard & Danielle Jouanny
Address: 22560 Trebeurden
Tel: (96) 23.57.26, telex: 740656
23 Rooms all with private bath
Moderate
Credit Cards: AX, VS

Secluded in a the residential hills of town is a very elegant and refined hotel. With only ten bedrooms, all which look out to the sea, the Manoir de Lan Kerrellec was once the private home of Monsieur Daube's grandparents. During the war it opened up to guests as a "salon de the", but, has perfected its qualities and services as a hotel over the past few decades. The circular dining room is truly spectacular with a high vaulted, wood ceiling and views out to a secluded section of the coast are unobstructed.

If you are traveling with children it is also interesting to note that two additional bedrooms, equipped only with a washbasin, are across from the larger rooms, and overlook the garden.

MANOIR DE LAN KERRELLEC
Hotelier: M. Daube
Address: 22560 Trebeurden
Tel: (96) 23.50.09
10 Rooms, Moderate
Open: 15 Mar to 29 Oct
Credit Cards: AX, CB
U.S. Rep: David Mitchell
Tel: (212) 696-1323 telex: 422123

Deep in the country, all you've passed for miles are cattle grazing, so where are you going to stop for the night? At a farmhouse - what could be more natural? Ferme and Restaurant, La Verte Campagne can offer you a delicious meal in a darling room with a cozy fireplace and comfortable accommodations. There are only eight rooms, most of them are quite small but then so is the price. In fact, I found the smaller they got the cuter they became. Room # 7 with two twin beds and bath and Room # 6 with a double bed and bath, are the largest of all the rooms. Room # 1 on the other end of the scale is the smallest, tiny in fact. It has a delicate pink print wallpaper and just enough room to sleep. Room # 3, one of the medium-sized rooms, is the one I liked most. It has one bed and is decorated with bright red and white checks.

LA VERTE CAMPAGNE
Hotelier: Mme Meredith
Address: Hameau Chevalier
Trelly, 50660 Quettreville
Tel: (33) 47.65.33
8 Rooms, Inexpensive
Open: All Year

Opening up on one side to farmland, this charming hotel also has its own darling little garden in back with a small stream and various small bridges.   The rooms have all recently been redone to perfection.   Everything matches down to the smallest detail.   Room #10 is in large red and white checks; the comforters, the pillows, the curtains, the canopy.   The restaurant is located in the barn and the tables are cleverly positioned within each of the stalls.

LE VIEUX LOGIS ET SES LOGIS DES CHAMPS
Hotelier: Mme Giraudel-Destord
Address: 24510 Tremolat
Tel: (53) 22.80.06 telex: 541025
23 Rooms, Moderate
Closed: January
Credit Cards: All Major
U.S. Rep: David Mitchell
Tel: (212) 696-1323 telex: 422123

TRIGANCE   Chateau de Trigance   Map# 105

In the middle of a beautiful valley with mountains towering as much as 5000 feet on either side, and the mouth of the Canyon of Verdun in the distance is the Chateau de Trigance.   The restorations involved in making this hotel can only be fully appreciated after seeing the before and after shots.   Additions are still being made. Construction of an extra six rooms will be started soon. At present there are only a few rooms, which are small, definitely not luxurious but nice with a medieval flavor. The restaurant is renowned for its fine cuisine. M and Mme Thomas are in charge of the hotel. But during the winter they return to the city and he again becomes a marketing expert while she works once more in publications for a cosmetic firm.

CHATEAU DE TRIGANCE
Hotelier: M et Mme Jean Claude Thomas
Address: 83142 Trigance
Tel: (94) 76.91.18
8 Rooms, Moderate
Open: Mar to Nov
Credit Cards: AX, VS
U.S. Rep: David Mitchell
Tel: (212) 696-1323 telex: 422123

| VALENCAY | Hotel D'Espagne | Map # 39 |

This marvelous villa near the Chateau de Valencay was once the hideaway for the exiled Spanish princes under Napoleon's command. Isolated and enchanting with its vine covered walls, cobbled courtyard, covered terrace bordered by beautiful flowers, gardens, and elegant rooms; it is still possible to make it your own secret hideaway. Since 1875, the gracious Fourre family have been welcoming guests into their home and serving them royally.

HOTEL D'ESPAGNE
Hotelier: Fourre Family
Address: 9 Rue Chateau
36600 Valencay
Tel: (54) 00.00.02 telex: 751675
10 Rooms, 8 Apt, Moderate
Open: 15 Mar to 15 Nov
Credit Cards: All Major
U.S. Rep: David Mitchell
Tel: (212) 696-1323 telex: 422123

VALENCE   Hotel-Restaurant Pic   Map# 116

In a region famous for its cuisine, Restaurant Pic still manages to stand out for its excellence.   There are only a few comfortable rooms but you'll be spending the majority of your time in the restaurant.   In summer, lunch and dinner are served in the shade of the garden.

HOTEL RESTAURANT PIC
Hotelier: M Jacques Pic
Address: 285 Avenue Victor Hugo
26000 Valence
Tel: (75) 44.15.32
5 Rooms, Moderate
Closed: August & 10 days in Feb.
Credit Cards: AX, DC
Restaurant: Closed Wed, & Sun evening

First, a beautiful, private drive winding up to this magnificent chateau and then to be met at the car with smiles and friendly greetings - my impression was set: Chateau de Castel Novel is a fantastic hotel! To top it off the cuisine is superb. (I have never had a more delicious soup, Veloute de Crepes).   The rooms are cozy, and excellently maintained.   The personnel became warmer and nicer as our stay progressed.   M Parveaux, Jr. is the handsome son of the present owners.   He has successfully built and opened the Hotel Prolong, a ski resort in Courchevel.   There are a relatively small number of rooms.   I found as they were shown to me that each one became my "favorite", in the order visited. They are all marvelous, but different.   Room #26 is great if you like to sleep in a turret; #19 has a set of magnificent wooden canopy beds; #16, the last room I'll mention, has two twin beds, two balconies and a lovely view.   There is also a beautiful pool.   I can't wait to return!   Chateau De Castel Novel is "oozing with charm."

CHATEAU DE CASTEL NOVEL
Hotelier: M Albert Parveaux
Address: 19240 Varetz
Tel: (55) 85.00.01 telex: 590065
28 Rooms, Very Expensive
Open: 1 May to 30 Oct
Credit Cards: AX, VS, Dc
U.S. Rep: David Mitchell
Tel: (212) 696-1323 telex: 422123
Pool, tennis

I was told to look for the largest tree in town and I would find myself at Auberge des Seigneurs!   Vence is a quaint little town and M P. Rodi has taken advantage of that fact and continued to spread charm throughout the hotel with lots of copper bed warmers and pans, wooden furniture, beautiful flowers, a large stone fireplace, old wooden doors, and cozy rooms.

SEIGNEURS ET DU LION D'OR
Hotelier: M Rodi
Address: Place Frene
06140 Vence
Tel: (93) 58.04.24
10 Rooms, Inexpensive
Open: 1 Dec to 15 Oct

VENCE   Chateau Saint Martin   Map # 114

Looking up from the town of Vence you can easily see, situated on the hillside only two miles away, the Chateau de Domaine Saint Martin.   It stands behind the historical ruins of an old drawbridge, tower and wall giving the hotel a feeling of the past, while a beautifully located swimming pool and tennis courts provide the pleasures of the present.

CHATEAU SAINT MARTIN
Hotelier: Mlle Brunet
Address: Rte Coursegoules
06140 Vence
Tel: (93) 58.02.02 telex: 470282
25 Rooms, Very Expensive
Open: 1 Mar to 25 Nov
Credit Cards: All Major
U.S. Rep: David Mitchell
Tel: (212) 696-1323 telex: 422123

| VEZAC | Manoir de Rochecourbe | Map # 54 |

Dordogne, perhaps my favorite region of France, seems to have an abundance of small country inns to choose from. Fortunately, or not, it is, however, difficult for me to isolate a favorite hotel as each has an individual style, charm and appeal. Since they each deserve special attention, the only solution I have arrived at is to make repeated visits to the Dordogne in the hopes of savouring them all! As a result, compounding the "problem", with each visit, I seem to happen upon just one more "gem". Such is the case with the discovery of the Rochecourbe, Manoir-Hotel. While staying at the hotel Bonnet, Mme Bonnet informed me that her sister had recently renovated a small manor into a few intimate, and luxurious accommodations. The dainty chateau with its one single turret belonged to Mme Roger's grandmother and most of the furnishings are original or from Monsieur Roger's family. Surrounded by its own lacey garden it seemed appropriate that each of the seven rooms was named after a flower. Climb the turret to your chamber. All the rooms are with adjoining bath with the exception of the littliest which has an adjacent shower but the w.c., although private, down the hall. Simple meals are prepared and served in a small and intimate dining room. This is indeed a unique and lovely manor-hotel, and the welcome is delightfully consistent and characteristic of the Bonnet Family.

MANOIR DE ROCHECOURBE
Hotelier: M et Mme Roger
Address: 24220 Vezac
Tel: (53) 29.50.79
7 Rooms, Moderate
Open: 1 Apr to 1 Nov
Credit Cards: AX

VEZELAY   Hotel Poste et Lion D'Or   Map# 144

Considered to be one of France's most picturesque villages, Vezelay is a must today just as it was in the Middle Ages when it was considered an important pilgrimage stop. Perched on the hillside overlooking the romantic valley of the Cousin, Vezelay is a wonderful place to spend the afternoon, enjoy a countryside picnic, or if afforded the luxury of time to linger and spend the evening in the confines of this medieval village. A popular choice for a hotel is the Poste et Lion D'Or. It is a hillside inn that sits at the exterior of the gates and walls to Vezelay. Poste et Lion d'Or is believed to have existed as a Relais de la Poste in the middle ages, accommodating those who either awaited the opening of the drawbridge or had just left the confines. Throughout the hotel there are still remembrances left from times more recent than the days of knights and armor. Flowers are planted in what were once troughs. Horses were hitched outside and it was custom for the innkeeper to provide free hay. The rooms in the main building are lovely and decorated with handsome antiques. The furniture has been collected piece by piece since the current owner's grandmother purchased the relais almost 60 years ago. The ivy-clad annex is surrounded by a sprawling english garden. The rooms are quiet but the decor was a bit modern. The restaurant, too, has so much potential and yet had an unusual mix of decorations. The Danguy family is on the premises to welcome you and skillfully manage this comfortable hillside inn.

HOTEL POSTE ET LION D'OR
Hotelier: Famille Danguy
Address: Place du Champ de Foire
89450 Vezelay
Tel: (86) 33.21.23 telex: 800949
42 Rooms, Moderate
Open: Easter to Nov
Credit Cards: AX, VS

VILLEFRANCHE SUR SAONE   Chateau de Chervinges   Map# 124

The Chateau de Chervinges is an elegant, adobe-wash country manor that lavishes in the ambiance of open fires, masses of flowers, charming decor and lovely accommodations. The service is refined and the location is ideal for touring the wine region of Beaujolais.

CHATEAU DE CHERVINGES
Hotelier: Roland et Huguette Legros
Address: Chervinges
69400 Villefranche Sur Saone
Tel: (74) 65.29.76 telex: 380772
12 Rooms, 6 Apt
Expensive
Closed: January & February
Credit Cards: AX, DC, VS

VILLENEUVE LES AVIGNON   La Magnaneraie   Map# 92

This hotel has now been open for almost a decade.   It is run by M (also the chef) and Mme Prayal and they create a very friendly and warm atmosphere.   There is a nice pool, attractive garden, a couple of cozy sitting rooms, darling restaurant and excellent menu that varies a little from day to day depending on what M Prayal picked up at the market.   The rooms are all nice with some excellent, while others are more on the simple side.   Room #10 was my favorite.   It had a double bed built on a wooden platform, bright cheerful wallpaper and a balcony that looked out over the garden.   There is also an apartment - Room #22 - which is away from the hotel with its own patio opening onto the garden.   Very attractive hotel.

HOSTELLERIE LA MAGNANERAIE
Hotelier: M et Mme Prayal
Address: 37, Rue Camp de Bataille
30400 Villeneuve les Avignon
Tel: (90) 25.11.11
21 Rooms, Moderate
Open: All Year
Credit Cards: All Major
Pool, Tennis, Park

VILLENEUVE LES AVIGNON   Le Prieure   Map# 92

The Priory, which had been constructed in 1322 on the orders of Cardinal Armand de Via, was purchased in 1943 by M Roger J. Mille who then transformed the property into a small and inviting hotel. A number of renovations and improvements have been made in the past few years. The "Chapitre" was completely remodeled and out of what used to be ten small rooms there are five lovely twins with bathrooms, and two lovely suites. The dining room has also been enlarged by moving the fireplace and adding large picture windows. Everything has been done with the refinement and taste that the Priory is known for. A beautiful pool and gardens surround the hotel, and the old furniture which is well preserved and still used, adds charm and beauty to this wonderful hotel.

LE PRIEURE
Hotelier: M Jacques Mille
Address: 7, Place de Chapitre
30400 Villeneuve les Avignon
Tel: (90) 25.18.20 telex: 431042
35 Rooms, Expensive
Open: 10 Mar to 10 Nov
Credit Cards: All Major
U.S. Rep: David Mitchell
Tel: (212) 696-1323 telex: 422123
Pool, tennis, park

VILLENEUVE LES AVIGNON   Vieux Moulin   Map # 92

Situated directly on the Rhone, this hotel, which before being converted was an old mill, serves delicious food and has a charming atmosphere. There are antiques everywhere, beamed ceilings, arched doorways, heavy wooden doors and cozy rooms.

HOSTELLERIE DU VIEUX MOULIN
Hotelier: M. Didier Gibellino
Address: Rue du Vieux Moulin
30400 Villeneuve les Avignon
Tel: (90) 25.00.26
22 Rooms, Inexpensive
Open: All Year
Credit Cards: AX, DC, EC

This wonderful hotel is located at the foot of the darling village of Villeray along the river in the heart of the Perche region.   Abandoned for nearly thirty years before conversion into a hotel, it was originally a mill and once served as a cheese factory.   The proud owners are especially nice and eager to please their guests.   The hotel has only ten rooms, each of which as its own individuality and name.   They include: Room #4, Louis XV done in a rustique decor; Room #5, Chambre Espanol in red/creme tones; Room #2 Baroque Venetian; Room #7 Napoleon; Room #8 is perfect for parents and child; Room #10 is an end corner room which is bright and cheery.   They all have enormous bathrooms and are very modern.   I also noticed bathrobes draped over the tubs, a nice added touch. There are views from each room overlooking the garden.   It has a central restaurant where delicious food will be served to you by waiters in native costume.

MOULIN DE VILLERAY
Hotelier: M et Mme Roland Coldeboeuf
Address: Villeray
61110 Condeau
Tel: (33) 73.30.22   telex: 171779
10 Rooms, Moderate
Open: 1 Feb to 30 Nov
Credit Cards: All Major

Just outside of Epernay, Hostellerie la Briqueterie is a newly built yet atmospheric hotel. The rooms are attractively decorated with copies of antiques. Bathrooms are brand new and very spacious and the restaurant has good food.

HOTEL LA BRIQUETERIE
Hotelier: Monsieur Guillon
Address: Vinay
51200 Epernay
Tel: (26) 54.11.22 telex: 830712
42 Rooms, Moderate
Open: All Year
Credit Cards: All Major

For four generations now, the Blanc family has managed a successful and lovely hotel. Particularly well known for its restaurant, there are also sixteen attractive rooms.

Hotelier: M et Mme Georges Blanc, Address: 01540 Vonnas, (Ain)
Tel: (74) 50.00.10, 16 Rooms, Moderate, Open: Feb-Nov

Index

Alphabetical Listing by Hotel Name

HOTEL	TOWN	MAP #		PAGE(S)
COUDREE, Chateau de	Sciez Bonnatrait	132		242
COULORGUES, Chateau de	Bagnols sur Ceze	94		142
CRO MAGNON, Hotel	Les Eyzies de Tayac	53		177
DAUPHIN, Hotel du	Honfleur	12		188
DEMEURE DES BROUSSES	Montpellier	81	65	209
DEUX ILES, Hotel (4e)	Paris	1		123
DUC, Le Moulin du	Moelan sur Mer	22	29	203
EMPEREUR, Relais de l'	Montelimar	95	106	206
ESPAGNE, Hotel D'	Valencay	39		252
EUROPE, Hotel D'	Avignon	91		141
EYNE, Auberge D'	Eyne	66		176
FERME ST SIMEON, La	Honfleur	12	16	187
FINES ROCHES, Host.	Chateauneuf du Pape	93		166
FLEURVILLE, Chateau de	Fleurville	126		180
FRENES, Hotel les	Montfavet	87		207
GORCE, Moulin de la	La Roche L'Abeille	43		231
GRAND ECUYER, Hotel du	Cordes	72	69	176
GRIFFONS, Hotel des	Bourdeilles	50		155
GUE DES GRUES, Aub. au	Gue des Grues	7		186
GUE PEAN, Chateau de	Monthou sur Cher	38		208
GUTENBERG, Hotel	Strasbourg	137		244
HAMEAU, Le	Saint Paul de Vence	113		237
HAUTS DE LOIRE, Dom.	Onzain	33		221
HOTEL, L' (6e)	Paris	1		125
IGE, Chateau d'	Ige	127		189
IMPERATOR, Hotel	Nimes	83	80 108	220
ISENBOURG, Chateau d'	Rouffach	134	111	232
JULES CESAR, Hotel	Arles	85		138
LAMELOISE, Hotel	Chagny	128		162
LANCASTER, Hotel (8e)	Paris	1		128
LAN KERRELLEC, Man. de	Trebeurden	19		249

HOTEL	TOWN	MAP #	PAGE(S)
PETIT COQ aux CHAMPS	Campigny	10	159
PIC, Hotel-Restaurant	Valence	116	253
PIGONNET, Hotel le	Aix en Provence	102	74 132
PONDERACH, Chateau de	Saint Pons	69	238
POSTE et LION D'OR	Vezelay	144	257
POSTE, Host. de la	Avallon	145	140
POSTE, Hotel de la	Beaune	129	149
PRAY, Chateau de	Amboise	32	134
PRIEURE, Hostellerie le	Bonnieux	99	75 154
PRIEURE, Le	Chenehutte les Tuffeaux	28	35 170
PRIEURE, Le	Villeneuve les Avignon	92	77 260
REGALIDO, La	Fontvielle en Provence	84	181
RESERVE, Chateau de la	Lissieu	121	193
RESERVE, Hotel la	Beaulieu	111	93 148
RETIVAL, Manoir de	Caudebec en Caux	11	161
RIGNY, Chateau de	Rigny	133	230
ROC, Le Moulin du	Champagnac de Belair	48	42 164
ROCHECOURBE Man. de	Vezac	54	256
ROCHEGUDE, Chateau de	Rochegude	97	231
ROCHEVILAINE, Dom. de	Muzillac	25	31 215
ROUMEGOUSE, Chateau de	Gramat	76	47 185
ROYAL CHAMPAGNE	Champillon	139	164
RUATS, Moulin des	Avallon	145	140
ST ANTOINE & La Reserve	Albi	71	133
SAINT JEAN, Chateau	Montlucon	41	209
SAINT LOUIS, Hotel (4e)	Paris	1	122
SAINT MARCEL, Chateau	Agen	59	132
SAINT MARTIN, Chateau	Vence	114	255
SAINT MICHEL, Host.	Chambord	35	163
SAINT SIMON, Hotel (7e)	Paris	1	127
SAINTE FOY, Hotel	Conques	77	55 175

Index by Hotel

"INN DISCOVERIES FROM OUR READERS"

Future editions of KAREN BROWN'S COUNTRY INN SERIES are going to include a new feature - a list of hotels recommended by our readers. We have received many letters describing wonderful inns you have discovered; however, we have never included them until we had the opportunity to make a personal inspection. This seemed a waste of some marvelous "tips". So we have started a file to be used in each forthcoming edition of our guide books which will be called "INN DISCOVERIES FROM OUR READERS".

If you have a favorite discovery you would be willing to share with other travellers who love to travel the "inn way" please let us hear from you and include the following information.

1. Your name, address and telephone number

2. Name, address, and telephone of "Your Inn"

3. Brochure or picture of inn (we cannot return photographs)

4. Written permission to use an edited version of your description

5. Would you want your name, city and state included in the book?

In addition to our current guide books which include hotels in France, England, Scotland, Wales, Switzerland, and Italy, we are now researching guide books for all of Europe and would appreciate comments on any of your favorites. The type of inn we would love to hear about are those with special "Olde Worlde" ambiance, charm, and atmosphere. We need a brochure or picture so that we can select those which most closely follow the mood of our guides. We look forward to hearing from you. Thank you very much!

ORDER FORM

If you have enjoyed this travel guide and would like to receive an additional copy or purchase other books in Karen Brown's travel series on country inns, the following books can be purchased in most major bookstores or ordered directly from the the publisher. These delightful volumes are all similar in style and format and include detailed countryside itineraries and a selective list of charming, atmospheric inns. Lavishly illustrated with original drawings and maps these guides enhance any travel library and make wonderful gifts.

....

PLEASE MAIL TO:

Name: _____ Street _____

City: _____ State _____ Zip _____

I AM ENCLOSING A CHECK TO COVER ($9.95 per copy plus $1.00 per copy postage and handling. California residents please include 6.5% tax)

_____ copies of FRENCH COUNTRY INNS & CHATEAU HOTELS

_____ copies of ENGLISH, WELSH & SCOTTISH COUNTRY INNS

_____ copies of SWISS COUNTRY INNS & CHALETS

_____ copies of ITALIAN COUNTRY INNS & VILLAS

_____ GIFT PACK, all four books at $30.00 plus postage

_____ Please send information on titles to be released

make checks out to:
TRAVEL PRESS
P.O. Box 1477
San Mateo, Ca. 94401

Following the tradition and flavor of other Travel Press publications *FOOTLOOSE* will tempt the countryside traveler to explore unique and interesting destinations. Published quarterly, each issue will whisk you off to some exciting corner of the world; highlight a newly discovered country inn; recommend an international restaurant and share some of their specialties; update gourmet and wine releases; keep you posted on some of the best travel bargains, tours and news items; review the current theater in London, Paris, New York and provide a calendar spotlighting international cultural events.

If you would like to subscribe or receive further information concerning *FOOTLOOSE*, please fill out and mail the form below.

....

———— I AM INTERESTED IN RECEIVING FURTHER INFORMATION ABOUT *FOOTLOOSE*.

Name: ————————————————————————

Address: ——————————————————————————

City: ———————————— *State:* ——— *Zip:* —————————

This guide is especially written for the individual traveller. However, should you be interested in having all the details of your holiday preplanned, Town and Country Travel Service designs tours to Europe for small groups using hotels with special charm and appeal. For further information on the Country Inn Holidays we offer, or for custom tours we can plan for your own group or club please call:

TOWN & COUNTRY TRAVEL SERVICE
16 East Third Avenue
San Mateo, CA. 94401

Within California 800 227-6734
Outside California 800 227-6733

KAREN BROWN has spent most of her life in the San Francisco Bay area where she now lives with her devoted German Shepherd, "Andy", in a cozy cottage surrounded by her collection of antiques. When nineteen Karen traveled to Europe where she wrote *French Country Inns and Chateau Hotels* - the first book in what has grown to be an extremely successful series on charming small European hotels. When not writing, Karen has worked as a travel consultant and as a tour guide to Europe. She loves skiing, hiking, cooking, and entertaining. Another hobby is languages. Karen speaks fluent French and German. Her real love though is exploring the world and although she has traveled extensively, staying in a wide variety of accommodations ranging from tents in the Himalayas to safari camps in Africa, her favorite abode is still the small country inn of Europe which she captures so delightfully in her books.

Notes